UNDER THE WIRE

ISBN 1-887982-49-3

Library of Congress Catalog Card Number 96-61843

First Edition-
Published by

WRANGLER PRESS
1150 River Lane
Riverton, WY 82501

Many of these stories were previously published in
The WRANGLER Horse and Rodeo News.

UNDER THE WIRE

A Collection of Cowboy Humor

Gary Hodgson

illustrated by Steve Aller

foreword by Echo Roy

WRANGLER PRESS
1996

This book is dedicated to my parents, Lester and Cleora Hodgson, who started me on the road to adulthood and to my wife, Sue, who is patiently waiting for me to complete the journey.

Foreword

If you're looking for a book loaded with sentimentality, romance, action or adventure, this isn't the one for you. However, if you're wanting to read something that's just plain fun—this is it.

UNDER THE WIRE isn't a volume you should attempt to read in one sitting. Rather, this is a book which should be absorbed in small doses, because Gary Hodgson addresses several facets of the cowboy culture, in his own singular style. Scattered throughout the following pages, you'll find a little bit of the whole shebang called cowboy and/or rancher. But, you'll mostly find joviality. Gary tends to look at life with a sense of humor. And he has an unusual and particular ability of finding it in almost any situation. That's what separates him from other writers, and what will separate this book from many others you'll bring home. This is a book you'll leave laying around so you can pick it up from time to time just to escape from the every day doldrums.

Joining Gary in his endeavor is Steve Aller, an accomplished Montana cowboy and artist. Gary said he sent his writings up to Steve, who in his own unique way interpreted in sketch. I found it kind of scary that two fellas can think so much alike. But, it makes for a winning combination. It's because of this blending, you'll enjoy every page of this publication — simply because what one of these artists doesn't think of, the other did.

As one of the "assistant editors" during the final stages of this process, I had a whole lot of fun reviewing the material to be included in this text. As a fellow writer, I'm please to report this is solid stuff the whole family can enjoy, from grandma on down. And as a friend, I salute Gary on this comical collage. UNDER THE WIRE had me grinning from beginning to end.

Echo Roy, Shoshoni, WY
Cowboy Poet
Author of ECHOES IN THE WIND

Gary Hodgson

Thousands of readers are already familiar with Gary's gift of writing about his experiences with horses, cattle and people in a humorous, easy to identify with style. His widely circulated Under The Wire column provided the title for this, his second book.

Even more familiar is his voice heard daily by over three million listeners who depend on his and Sue's Livestock News Radio Network.

Gary and Sue operate a ranch in Brush, Colorado. they have four children, two grandchildren, two dogs and enough horses and cattle to keep Gary in stories for years to come.

He devotes every free moment (some he should have been working) to his passion, calf roping.

Steve Aller

Steve Aller and wife Jean, along with children Jordan and Reed, operate Boulder River Guest Ranch started by Steve's grandfather, Walter, near Mcleod, Montana in 1914.

Steve has been drawing and painting since childhood. His main interest has been painting and fine art, but he has always been known for his cartoons. He possesses an uncanny ability to read one of Gary's stories and draw exactly what most readers are envisioning.

Steve's other interests, in his own words, include "a poor golf game and raising and showing over-priced Quarter Horses."

A Wave of Friendship

Want to win friends? Be popular? Have everyone like you? Want to have people wave to you as you drive down almost any road in the country? It's easy. Just drive a pickup truck.

That's right, it's just that simple. Trade off that four door sedan. Scrap the station wagon. Go get yourself a pickup to drive and you will instantly have all the afore mentioned things happen to you.

Present pickup drivers know what I'm talking about, already. Those of you who have never wheeled up and down the turnpike in a pickup probably are still skeptical. The truth is, though, when you drive around in a pickup everyone seems to like you. They wave. Yep, start down any road in the country in a pickup and people will wave to you as they drive past. Generally, they too, are driving a pickup.

DEKAL
STEVE ALLER
'96

It seems to be generally understood that if you are driving a pickup, you wave to other pickups on the highway. There seems to be an undeclared fraternity of pickup drivers. Maybe there are rules in the owners manual that comes with a new pickup on this. Page 93, section seven, "in order to keep the warranty valid on you new vehicle, remember to wave at all passing fellow pickup drivers."

I'm not sure of this because I've never owned one new enough to still have the owner's manual in it.

Whenever I drive my pickup, no matter whether it's around my home town or on a country road four states away, people wave as they pass.

I haven't decided if it's because they are thinking "No one would drive that thing far from home. He must be a neighbor so I'd better wave." Or if their thoughts are, "He drives a pickup so he must be OK." In any event, as you pass, you get a wave.

Sometimes drivers of cars wave, too. I figure those must be people who normally drive pickups and just wave out of habit. They may be saying, "Hey, I'm really OK too, but today I'm just in this car."

Now not all pickups seem to be in this

unofficial brotherhood. Pickups rolling around with huge oversize tires and florescent pink windshield wipers don't seem to belong. Maybe they wave to each other but they don't seem to make the drivers eligible for the regular membership. Little compact pickups may or may not participate. Their drivers seem to say, "Look, I'm not proud of this 1/2 size imitation of a real pickup but I'm on my way home to get my 3/4 ton right now so I can do some serious waving."

There are ways to add even more to your popularity on the road. To get more waves yet, put a few bales of hay in the back. Another sure fire wave getter is to wear a cowboy hat (no feathers, please) or a seedcorn cap. (Can they really tell passing you at sixty miles per hour? ...YOU BET!) The best way of all to insure waves? Hook a horse or stock trailer to the back of your pickup. I guarantee more waves per mile. I'll see you on the highway!

Horsin' Around

Want to buy or sell cattle? Give me a call. Want to buy or sell a horse? I'm not home.

That's right, I want to advertise that I'm not in the horse tradin' business. Strange, huh? Not at all.

Most of my life has been spent buying or selling cattle in one capacity or another. Thousands of dollars have been transacted by phone, handshake or verbal contract. People buy loads of cattle sight unseen. No problem. But horses ... No Sir.

There is something special about horses that affects people's good judgement. The man who would purchase 110 black cows sight unseen over the phone for $900 each and be happy about it, will not buy an $800 horse until looking at it, riding it, taking it home, bringing it back and taking it home again.

In the cow transaction he might say "They bred?" You answer, "You bet," and you have a deal. In the horse transaction he says, "I want a panel of various vets, trainers and other experts to evaluate his conformation, disposition and pedigree. Then if the psychologist says his personality is compatible with the wife's, "I'll take him home for a week trial."

I'd like to tell him no creature has a personality compatible with his wife's, but I keep still.

If you sell someone a calf and a week later it dies, you never hear a word about it. Sell someone a horse and five months later it comes up with a sore knee, he calls wanting his money back.

You can sell feeder steers all day long without a problem. Try to sell one horse and you have lots of problems.

Either his color doesn't match the saddle pad they just bought, he objects to having one leg held up for five minutes (I would, too!) or he just seems a little nervous around the kids. (Their kids make me nervous, too. I predict they'll be in reform school before the horse gets rode anyway.)

So if you've got a horse to sell or want to buy one, please remember my name and phone number and please don't call it!

Why I Don't Farm

I'm telling you right here and now, I am not a farmer. I even farmed for awhile once...just to prove to my neighbors I wasn't a farmer!

Now don't misunderstand me, there's absolutely nothing wrong with the profession. I actually envy those who can plant straight rows, care for mother nature's land and harvest bountiful crops to feed our nation. I just ain't one of them.

It's not that I dislike the work; in fact, I actually enjoyed most farming jobs. It is the equipment that I dislike. Swathers, balers, plows and especially tractors leave me in a cold sweat. Just like a horse, they can sense when I'm uncomfortable with them and that's when they act up.

I'll admit that as a pup growing up on my father's place, I wasn't always exposed to the most modern equipment available. We weren't exactly on the leading edge of technological developments on the Hodgson rancho. In fact, I remember how excited I was when we got a hay rake that had rubber tires. Our "bale wagon" came equipped with hay hooks and a set of denim hay chaps to wear. The steel seat of our old International "C" tractor left a permanent crease in my behind that makes it hard for me to sit on a tractor even today.

It seems like whenever I touched a tractor, something broke. Admittedly, I did tend to daydream out there driving from one end of the field to the other, back and forth, hour after hour. Maybe I should have been paying more attention when the harrow came up over the rear wheel of the tractor as I turned too short or when the disk came unhooked from the tractor up at the other end of the field. It was sort of a shock to turn the tractor around at the end of the field and find the disk I thought I was pulling, setting there to meet me head-on in the middle of the field!

I suppose my dad was right when he said the mower was supposed to cut the hay, not plug up and drag it down. (He also said some other stuff about where I must of had my head, but I won't go into that here!).

STEVEHALLER
'96

It wasn't just my father who I failed to please with my machinery skills. I worked for a good man who put me on a tractor cultivating sugar beets. Once. After creeping through the field watching six rows of tiny beets coming through the shields, I guess my mind wandered a little. A quarter of a mile later, I discovered no little beets were coming through the shields any more! Six rows had suddenly gotten "cultivator blight" and disappeared. My job also disappeared soon thereafter.

My trouble is I was born fifty years too late. I would have done better with a horse drawn implement. At least with a horse and I out in the field there would be one brain working.

Help Wanted: Rodeo Secretary

"Hello, are you the man who advertised in the newspaper for a rodeo secretary?"

"Yep, sure am. When can you start?"

"Start? Wait a minute, you haven't even asked me for my resume. Don't you want my previous references and employment history? Aren't there any requirements for this job?"

"Are you breathin' regular?" the male voice asked.

"Well of course I am", the female stammered, "But..."

"You got one good arm to write with and at least one eye you can see out of?" he continued.

"Yes, but..."

"Then you got the job. I need someone, anyone, right now," the man said with a hint of desperation in his voice.

"Why are you so desperate?" she asked.

"Wouldn't just about any gal love to work around all those hunky cowboys amid the excitement of a rodeo?"

"You've never been around a rodeo office before, have you?" the interviewer asked.

"Well, no, but it must be fun!" she replied.

"Yeah, right" the man answered. "Bleary eyed cowboys, tired from too much driving, mad about turn out fees and late callback charges, wanting to get traded, waited on first...and occasionally needing a shower real bad. It's a girl's dream all right. Can you work long hours for poor pay? Take the blame for everything! Be told nothing, yet be expected to answer everybody's questions?"

"Gee, it sounds rough," the caller murmured, "What about working conditions?"

"Oh, they vary somewhat from a card table behind the chutes to an unair-conditioned room at one end of the concession stand, generally near the stove."

"Why in the world would anyone want that job?" the young lady caller asked.

"Darned if I know, but we're all just really glad there are some who will do it."

"Ditto."

What I Really Mean...

Having spent much of my life in and around Rodeo, I have been on a constant search for the perfect horse. Now, I am not a horse trader. Never have been, will never be one. My business philosophy has been ... give too much, then sell for too little.

Over the years I have, however, learned a few things I want to pass on to other horse buyers and sellers.

Here is a glossary of terms as they tend to be used in the world of horse trading:

Heeling Horse -

1. Can't run fast enough to be the first one to the steer.
2. Too small to do anything else.
3. (variation) Should be totally (healed) up by now so we can sell him.

Heading Horse -

1. Won't stop unless some one drops an anchor (or heels the steer).
2. Too big to do anything else.
3. (variation) Also been heeled on - really isn't good at either.

Calf Horse -

1. Has pulled back and broken many head stalls (works lots of rope).
2. Stops good (couldn't get dallies for heeling).
3. (variation) Been heeled on, doesn't stop real good.

Youth Horse -

1. Small
2. Old
3. Slow

Amateur Horse -

1. Big
2. Old
3. Slow

Prospect -

1. Young
2. Slow
3. May be big or small

Halter Prospect -

Pretty but keeps bucking us off.

BIG SALE
HORSES FOR SALE
STEVE ALLER
96

Needs a cowboy to ride him - Watch out!
That cowboy probably needs to be Ty Murray.

Been "ranched on" -
Takes about 400 acres to stop or turn him around.

Anyone can ride him -
Hundreds have tried.

Just needs riding -
Oh, boy!

Professionally trained -
Going to cost a lot!

Older Kid's horse -
If he gets bucked off he wasn't old enough.

Been roped off some - Didn't like it much.

The world of horse trading is full of original thinkers coming up with ways to make you look forward to what this horse is about to do to you. This does provide us all with a way to pass the time during the off-months when there are not very many rodeos or horse activities to go to. The horse trader does provide a very useful service, however. Not only does he keep coming up with these amazing buys, he also purchases our mistakes and provides you and me with a source of entertainment.

It's A Dog's World

There's a new addition at the Hodgson Ranch. That's right, tiny footsteps can be heard around the hacienda.

It's not what you think. These footsteps are made by four fuzzy paws. Yep, a puppy has taken over our household. We sleep when she says it's time and the whole family gets up when this ore pound bully says to.

This newest dog, if you can call the little motorized fur ball a dog, got me to thinking of past dogs in our life. This one is a house dog, she'll never help out in the corrals. Most of the others were cow dogs. Now that I think of it, they didn't help out much in the corrals either!

Jake was a genuine dingo cow dog. Jake could run up and down the feed alley and keep four hundred calves from feed and water just for fun in his spare time. During working hours, if you could call them that, you could count on Jake to always be in the wrong place. After trying to drive two hundred calves thru a gate for five minutes only to have them all turn and run back over five cowboys, there was Jake standing smack dab in the middle of the gate. He never let one slip past him.

Another dog was a female border collie that was waiting for me in the back of my pickup one day when I came out of the local auction. She had decided she would go home with me and snarled when I tried to get her out. What could I do, I was adopted!

I named her Founder cause that's where she came from. The name got me into a number of "who's on first" routines with people a little confused between her name and how I got her.

"Nice dog," they'd say, "where did you get her?"

"Found her," I'd say.

"Oh, you did? Well, what's her name?"

"Founder," I'd answer.

"Yea, you said you'd found her. What's her name?"

"Founder," I would insist.

"Look, I don't really care how you got her, what's her name?"

"Founder," I'd persist.

"She ever wander off?" they'd ask.

"Yep."

"When you went looking for her what did you yell out?"

"Founder."

"I mean before you found her. What did you call out?"

"Founder."

"Look, I can see you found her. Otherwise she wouldn't be here now. But if she was lost, who would you look for?"

"Founder."

"I know you found her but before then."

"Founder."

"Oh, never mind."

Then there was Potsey, a blue tick lab mix. He liked to chase cars but never learned to dodge them. He must have gotten run over six or eight times. Each time he'd heal up and go after them again. Finally he had to pack a back leg around. He could run twenty miles per hour on three legs but used the fourth for a sort of overdrive. At twenty, he'd put it down and get about five more miles per hour out of it.

Well, this latest mutt has quite a legacy to live up to. Guess she'll start as soon as she finishes chewing up the pair of two hundred dollar boots I just noticed her working on.

"Quit that!"

What Do You Know?

It's been said that there are two things a cowboy knows nothing about...cows and horses. There is only one thing a cattleman knows nothing about... the cattle market.

I'm not talking about just a few cattlemen, I'm talking about anyone and everyone who has anything to do with the cattle business. It makes no difference if you're on a ranch, feedlot, auction or a custom manure hauling franchise. It makes no difference even if your job is reporting the markets as mine is... no one can understand the cattle market.

Think about it. We spend hours pouring over futures, fats, auction results and dressed meat trade figures. We even follow shadowy figures like the "estimated box beef cutout" data. Yet, if you really know anything about the markets after all that, please step forward.

We study. We analyze. We estimate and theorize. When it's all over, the markets still surprise us. Nobody knows what the markets will do.

A great philosopher (maybe not so great, for all I know) once said, "To know the past is to understand the future." He (or she) obviously never followed the cattle markets.

We gather data, chart trends, study reports and make predictions. These activities are generally followed by statements like, "Well, I'll be darned!" When the exact opposite occurs in the market.

Now, don't feel bad if you are one of the people I'm talking about. If you have been on the family ranch for five generations of raising cattle and still don't seem to be able to predict markets, don't feel like anyone is picking on you.

Some of us spend most of our time each and every day of the year gathering, studying and/or reporting livestock market news. The markets are our job and when it gets down to the nitty gritty, we don't understand them any more than anyone else. As a matter of act, if someone tells you he's got the markets all figured out, just politely agree and slowly move away from him. You don't want to get tangled in the net when the boys from the funny farm come for him.

I occasionally have been asked to predict the market. I generally tell them I know nothing about the cattle business and have the check book to prove it!

A friend just yesterday asked me if I thought a storm would blow in this weekend as predicted. I told him I didn't know a thing about the weather so I couldn't predict it.

My job is not knowing anything about the cattle markets.

SOME FUTURES
STEVE ALLER
96

I'm Sorry

The other day my wife, Sue, and I had a little spat. Well, truth is we had a big spat. You guys know the kind. The kind where you can't win. Even if you can win, you lose, so you just go ahead and lose.

The trouble is, even when you go ahead and lose an argument with your wife that still ain't enough. I suppose in countries where it's considered appropriate to cut off a finger to show grief or remorse, that serves as enough, but here in the good ole U.S. that sort of thing just isn't allowed. Lucky for me or I'd only be able to count on my fingers to about four by now. Anyway, I needed to get this thing patched back up somehow. My wife had to know I was sorry and finger cuttin' was out.

There was only one solution to this situation. That's right...flowers and a card. So off to town

I went to buy me some forgiveness. Now, the flowers were no problem. I had six dollars left in my checking account after stopping at the feed store so, darn it, I just spent it all at the flower store. Now that I had a dozen three day old carnations the next stop was the drug store for the appropriate card.

"May I help you?, " the sales clerk asked.

"Well, ma'am, I need a card for my wife," I said.

"Birthday or anniversary?" she asked.

"Neither," I answered, really not wanting to go into it in much detail.

"Well, what do you want to say?" she persisted.

"Sorry," I said kind of under my breath.

"Sorry about what?" the lady pressed.

I suspected her own curiosity had exceeded her professional interest by now.

"About the chain saw."

"The what?" she asked.

"The chain saw," I figured I'd better go on and tell her the whole story.

"You see I brought my chain saw into the kitchen to clean it up. I left it sitting on the floor she'd just mopped and all the oil and gas ran out on the floor."

"Sounds serious," the clerk observed.

"Naw, that wasn't bad. Then her dog came through and walked in the stuff and tracked it across her new carpet."

"Oh dear." she added.

"Oh, that wasn't the worst. This was the day her ladies club was coming to visit and they all showed up just as she came out of the bedroom from getting dressed and saw the situation. She got plumb P.O.ed."

"Well, sir," the helpful clerk beamed, "I've got just the right card for the situation." She handed me a card.

"What's it say?" I asked.

"Oh, it doesn't matter," she smiled, the important thing is that you mail it from three states away!"

Tomorrow's Museum

The year is 3090. The tour guide is conducting a tour of the ancient farm implement museum in Washington, D.C. He was winding his way through the rows of long idled 4020s, 4 wheel drive Chevys and Hesston big balers.

"How primitive things were in those days," a lady remarked looking at a 1990 vintage corn planter.

"I don't see how they were able to do anything with this stuff," a man observed standing in front of a John Deere 4440 tractor with wrap around cab.

"On this specimen, please notice the crude repairs done with the unusual material," the tour guide pointed out.

"Ooooh - Awww," the crowd murmured. "What in the world is that stuff wrapped all over the parts like that?" a man asked.

MUSEUM
STEVE ALLEN
96

"It was called baling wire, although we're not sure how it got that name. We have found many, many examples of its use on this early day machinery. It was used a lot like the rawhide the even earlier inhabitants of the West used to repair things."

"What an odd name," a lady snickered, "and look how much of it they used."

"That's right," the guide answered. "It seems to have been extremely plentiful for a very long period of time. We have found traces of it even on very new machinery. It seemed to be some sort of ritual to add it to any new machine purchased."

"How odd!" a little girl laughed.

"Even stranger is the rest of the story concerning this baling wire. In the late 1980's it suddenly vanished."

The crowd gasped.

"That's right, it just disappeared from the face of the earth. These late 1980 model machines even seemed to have old wire used on them. There appears to have been no more new baling wire available. Scientists have theorized that either production of it was ruled illegal by the government or some exotic disease destroyed all the makers of the stuff. In any event, just like the Carrier Pigeon, the dinosaur, the raving environmentalist, and the Inca Indians, baling wire just ceased to exist. We have here in our museum some of the finest examples of its usage anywhere. Most of these samples come from an archeological site found near what used to be Brush, Colorado. We refer to these ancient ruins as the 'Hodgson Place'. This seems to have been the name of a tribe that lived there at one time."

As the awestruck crowd moved along to the next exhibit, the guide pointed to a shiny metallic object about four inches long and 3/4 inches in diameter in a show case.

"This unusual object has some strange power that attracts metal objects to stick to it. This device was called a cow magnet for some odd reason. By a bizarre coincidence it seemed to also have ceased to exist at about the same period that the baling wire disappeared."

"Now, if you will follow me into our next area, we'll see our exhibit of what appears to be cow chips covered with plastic. Some even have ancient ball point pens sticking from them."

Rodeo School

A big part of being a successful rodeo competitor is talent, but an even bigger ingredient is desire. To succeed in rodeo you've got to have a big chunk of "want to" in your heart.

There are schools that teach you skills and help "would be" contestants develop their talent. There was no way to teach good old down -in- your- soul desire.

Until now, that is.

Plan now to attend the first ever Gary Hodgson School of True Rodeo Desire. The first classes have already begun but we're still accepting applicants.

By now you are probably wondering how we plan to teach you "try". It's easy, just move to Colorado in the winter time. Or, you may move to Wyoming, Nebraska, Montana or anyplace where ear flaps start to replace straw hats around

November first. Now, once you've established residency in one of these northern latitudes, just keep on rodeoing. That's when the real "try" comes out in a person. Anyone who wants to pursue his or her interests in rodeo through the winter months will get a real education on desire.

Anyone who lives in the cold part of the country knows what I'm talking about. You have to have riding or roping burning in your heart fiercely to keep on going thru the winter. In fact, without that fire burning in you, you'll probably freeze your Fruit of the Looms off!

It use to be that most of the good ropers came from the south because of the warmer year around weather. Fine, if you wanted to rope year around, you moved south. Then some poor misguided soul invented the indoor arena. Heralded as the great equalizer between north and south, it in fact created hardships far beyond it's creators imagination. Now instead of staying inside until spring watching old NFR tapes and talking about Arizona, those of us bitten with the rodeo bug had an alternative.

Wonderful. Now we find ourselves putting on long handles, mittens, ear flaps and layers of shirts and going out to rope and ride. True, the buildings provide semi-protected places to practice our skills but they are seldom comfortably warm; they don't keep the ice off the roads leading to them, the hair off our horses, nor snow balls from forming on the horse's feet.

While I don't know of any research into the subject, I'll bet bull riders bones break easier when it's zero outside than when it's 85 degrees. I'll bet broncs lean on the side of the chute harder when they are carrying their winter hair and fat than they do in their sleek, slimmed down July form.

In short, rodeoing in the winter in the north half of the country is tough. This toughness s the foundation for my new rodeo "try" school. If you can remain active from November until the end of March, you will get to be tough and you will have developed a real big lump of "want-to" inside.

Like all good schools we have a room and board package available. You can come live here on our place. Our conditioning program will get you in shape, too. It includes snow shoveling, walking everywhere wearing ten pounds of clothes plus five buckle overshoes and carrying large amounts of hay and grain to stock who's pasture is under a foot of snow.

If, during the five month session, students have any questions they are free to call me. I'll leave the number where I can be reached in Arizona. You see, I'll be down there developing a similar school for all those southern cowboys on how to rodeo during the months of June, July and August.

WEATHER
ROCK
STEVE ALLER
'96

Weather Rock

As I drove into the ranch gate and across the cattleguard I saw it. A large flat rock suspended by chains from a tripod stood next to the gate. A sign nearby identified it as the "weather rock".

As I drove down the lane to the ranch my mind ran back again and again to the rock. "Weather rock", huh. It looked old and authentic. It could just be a joke but then again it might be legitimate.

I knew the rancher I was going to see fairly well. They were good folks but I didn't have them pegged for big jokers. Surely they wouldn't go to all that trouble to create a trap for poor unsuspecting visitors.

On the other hand the area was full of history and Indian lore. In a land of arrow heads, tepee rings and ancient artifacts, this "weather rock" could be a re-creation of a historic sight. I'd heard of the "council tree", Indian burial grounds and other traditional gathering places of the past inhabitants of the west.

Then again, if it was put up as a joke for city visitors, I certainly wasn't going to fall for the joke. No sir. I would just play it cool and not mention it at all.

The purpose of my visit was to help work some cows I'd just sold them. Throughout the day our tasks were preg checking, vaccinating and ear tagging cows. My hands did the motions but my mind was on that darn rock hanging from the tripod.

I waited for them to lure me into a conversation about it.

"Nice day, huh?" Frank asked.

"Yup," I replied. Thought you'd draw me in didn't you? Well you can't fool old Gar.

By the end of the day that stone had become an obsession with me. I couldn't help it, I had to ask. I was beaten by curiosity.

"OK, Frank, what's the deal on the weather rock out by your gate?" I sheepishly asked.

Straight faced at first he answered, "It works perfectly. You can tell the weather from it. If the stone is wet, it's raining. If it's hot the sun is shining. When it swings from the chain, the wind is blowing. Never missed once." As he ended his explanation he broke into the same fits of laughter the rest of the crew were already in.

Curiosity may have killed the cat, but it sure made a fool of me!!

Quality Time

This is the story that almost didn't get written. I had a good reason, though. I had to clean the barn.

Some days I would rather clean the barn than write. Some days I would rather mow the lawn than balance my checkbook. Some days I just seem to long for a job that takes little thought or at least doesn't come with responsibilities and worries.

I'll bet than many of you have those same feelings some days. "I don't want to be a chief, just give me one of the Indian's jobs, today," is a thought we've all had occasionally. Today, I don't want to deal with banks, insurance forms, employees or anything else where I have to make a heavy decision. Just give me a simple task, then leave me and my daydreams alone for a few hours.

Now, don't misunderstand me. I really like my job and I like writing this column. It's just that some days spring fever sets in. My spring fever hits in almost any month of the year, however.

Many of you out there experience a double whammy on these kinds of days. Not only don't you get to do the kind of job you'd like to be doing but you have to hire someone else to do it while you must do something else less desirable.

How many of you have had to hire someone to run the new swather while you had to meet with the banker? Have any of you secretly desired to live the life of a cowboy and spend your days on top of a good horse out in the solitude of a good cattle range? Instead, many of us have to hire someone to do that job while the "boss" has to deal with the wonders of a Worker's Comp program or figuring a cash flow sheet for the P.C.A.!

A little saying I heard a long time ago says something about running a railroad. It sort of said, "I don't get to run the engine or ring the bell or blow the whistle." I don't get to yell 'All Aboard'. I don't even get to drive the spikes that hold the lines together. Yet, let one darn thing go wrong with the train and see who catches all the flack."

Cleaning the barn is dusty, dirty work. I could probably give one of the neighbor kids five dollars to do it. Then, though, they'd get to see how nice it looks freshly swept and raked clean. They'd get to smell the fresh shavings. They'd get to talk to the animals as they worked away.

Well folks, I wasn't about to let some little neighbor kid have all that fun. No Sir! Let him grow up and get his own barn. I hope if he does get one, that he'll have a chance to clean it every once in awhile. We all deserve a little quality time!

Rodeo Lingo

I, like many of you, have spent my lifetime in and around the world of horses and rodeo. That constant exposure to these things have had a pronounced effect on who we are. It affects the way we dress and even the way we talk. If you stop to think about it, our speech is so affected by our interest in rodeo that we now have our own language. Explaining that language to an outsider can get frustrating.

Suppose it was your job to teach a class on horse and rodeo language to a group of people. It might go like this...

"O.K. Today, class, we are going to present phrases and words common to the horse and rodeo world. The first one is, "Cracked Out". In the world of rodeo this means to begin as in "I cracked out in the saddle bronc last year."

"Teacher, teacher," little Johnnie asks. "Is that the same as broke out?"

"No, Johnnie. If you break out, you start too soon. Also, you only can break out in the timed events. In the rough stock events you have to mark-em-out which means you can't start until the horse does. I'm talking about spurring licks, here."

"What's that Johnnie? Licking your spurs? No, no. I'm talking about a spurring a pattern. Up in the fuzz for a bareback, front to back on a saddle bronc."

"No, Jannie, barrel racers don't spur a cloverleaf pattern. They run their horses in that pattern around the barrels."

"No, not the barrel with the clown in it. That one is out there for the bulls to run into. In the bull fights, a clown gets more points for getting the bull to hit the barrel."

"No, Jannie, the barrel racer doesn't get three times as many points for hittin' her barrels as the clowns do. Let's just move on to the next question."

"Yes, Ma'me, cowboys do flank roping calves. Next question?" "How do cowboys flank the bulls and bronc's? And why do they do it in the chute where no one can see?"

"Well, students. I'm sorry, but our time is up today. Tomorrow we'll get into how the judges draw an animal for each contestant. Do not bring crayons, please."

Don't Call Me "Pig Boy"

It has been said there are only two things a cowboy knows nothing about. Those two things are cows and horses. Let me add a third thing to the list ...PIGS.

This all started out one calm Wednesday morning as I sat in my studio office in the rear of the house and Sue was working in her office in the front of the house. (This separation of working areas is a "whole-nother" story to be covered later.)

Suddenly I heard her yell out, "Gary, there is a pig on the front porch!"

I was really surprised because none of my friends were expected by that morning, but before I could get up to go to the door, she hollered, "There's two, no three of them!"

I knew something was up because I couldn't remember having three friends but I went to the door anyway. As I opened the front door there stood three little white pigs staring at me.

Now I am NOT setting you up for a fairy tale. Honest to goodness, there were three baby pigs on my front step! When they saw me they took off running. (Sue said even pigs have standards.) They promptly ran right thru our horse corrals causing commotion like you've never seen. Our horses had never seen a pig and weren't too happy about their first one. It became obvious we had better catch these porkers before we had serous problems.

Suddenly a design flaw in our corral construction became apparent. Our fences were built to contain horses, calves and steers, not ten pound pigs. The only area fenced tight enough was our backyard. It is fenced "5-pound poodle proof". After a few tense moments, Sue and I got the pigs out of the horse pens and up into the back yard. Surprisingly they seemed perfectly content and stretched out on the lush lawn to nap.

We then began to try to figure where they had come from. We called every neighbor we could think of. Several have horses, a few cattle, even a sheep or two but NO pigs. These little critters couldn't have traveled very far, so we had a real mystery on our hands.

In the meantime the three little pigs had made themselves at home in our backyard. As I gazed at the sight of them grunting and exploring around my carefully mowed lawn, I wasn't too proud of the sight. It had sort of a "Beverly Hillbillys" look to it.

"Oh, well, who would ever know anyway," I thought.

I had no sooner had that thought than in drove our veterinarian. His eyes went immediately to the "pig pen" but he carefully avoided saying anything ... at least until he made his next stop. During the day, just about everyone I have ever known just happened to stop by, each with a remark or worse, silence, regarding how hard up the Hodgsons were getting that they were raising hogs in the backyard.

As the next few days wore on it became obvious we had to do something when no owner came forth. Truth is, we had kind of gotten used to them. Finally, we decided on a plan. We'd build a special pen for them down at the bottom of our arena, buy some grain and fatten us some pigs!

The thought of our own bacon, ham and pork chops started to sound like a good idea. In just a few months we could have turned our embarrassment into a full freezer. We even started to make plans for a big barbecue to share our good fortune with the neighbors.

On the fifth day of our venture into the hog business, everything changed. Into our yard drove a neighbor, who had been gone for a few weeks, with three sad-faced kids in tow.

"I hear you've got our pigs," she said.

Almost sadly we turned potential hams and bacon over to the now beaming kids.

Feeling the mother needed some explanation of our disappointment, I sheepishly explained our plans to surprise the neighborhood with a pig roast.

"Oh, dear!" she said, "I'm glad you didn't. You see, these are pot bellied pigs, they're two years old and this is as big as they'll ever get!"

Truth In Packaging

It was bound to happen, the 'Truth In Packaging' Law has been enacted, requiring manufacturers to label products with the contents contained inside. Now we will know exactly what the percentage of corriente steer is in those hot dogs.

I am a little concerned, however, that this trend may continue into other areas that will eventually affect the sport of rodeo.

In a few short years we may see old el toro in the bull riding, not only carrying a hot iron brand or two, but also a contents label. I can just see it now, right there on the crest of his neck, where the 'user' can read it as he places his bull rope...

Contents: (In order of importance)

Brahma 31%

Jersey Milk Cow 23%

Alligator 15%
Water Moccasin.............................. 5%
Other ingredients or additives:
Hay, oats, nitroglycerin, ugly pills . 25%
Minor traces of fly spray, the hip
pocket off a pair of Wrangler
jeans and red grease paint
from an unidentified origin............. 1%

This bull contains 100% of the RDA (Recommended Daily Allowance) of the following needs of a bull rider: fear, pain and adrenalin. Will also provide lesser amounts of income, girls and job re-training.

Now, if this 'contents' thing ever gets linked to government warnings on certain packages, we will probably find labels like these:

Roping Calf: Warning, this calf contains a high percentage of Louisiana Flop Ear. Users are warned he may break slow, run hard to the left, meet you 1/2 way up the rope and kick until he hears the whistle.

Dogging Steer: Warning, the third run on this steer usually results in a dental bill for the contestant.

I suppose this thing could go all the way to the contestants themselves. The numbers passed out to the cowboys could have a label attached, also. It might read...

Contents: Free spirit 42%
Determination 18%
Orneriness 5%
Kindness....................................... 10%
Respect 10%
Good sense 3%
Job Security 01%

Plus equal amounts of: Humor, honesty, dedication and humility.

In certain packages you may find some of the following: McDonald's hamburgers, aspirin, coffee, other beverages (unlisted) and Ben Gay Deep Heating Ointment.

That's right, folks, "Truth in Packaging" is going to change the face of rodeo, mark my words.

Note: contents of this story contain equal parts of:

Hot Air

B.S.

Panic over editor's deadline

Desire to keep from getting a real job

The Selection Process

"Maude, we've got to talk,'' Rancher Harry said to his wife, looking over the top of his newspaper. "That's right, Harry, we've got something very important to talk about,'' Maude answered. "It's about this young man our daughter is going to marry."

"We've got to buy a new bull pretty soon," Harry went on, apparently ignoring Maude. "I just don't know which one to buy. I've worried about this for months and the time is getting near for us to make the decision."

"His hair is long and he wears an earring," Maude continued. "He doesn't seem to have a job and he's always broke."

"That's nice," a preoccupied Harry muttered back as he read further. "We've got to decide on a breed to select first. Do we want the 'maternal breed', the gentle breed, the large breed, the right color or the 'carcass breed'?"

"He seems nice enough," Maude persisted, "But he wore shorts and sandals to the community picnic last week. He just didn't fit in."

"Oh yea?" Harry answered, really not hearing. "And after we decide on a breed, then we've got to decide whose sale to attend. There must be fifty advertised right here in this paper alone."

"Your daughter says this young man wants to continue on in school after they get married. Maybe five or ten more years. She'll have to work to support them both," Maude tried to slip in.

Totally engrossed in his problem, Harry went on, "Then we've got to consider EPD's, WDA's, fertility evaluations, and structural soundness. We've got to look at birth weights, calving ease and muscle score. I've got so many figures floating around in my head I don't know what to do. I've laid awake nights worrying about this until I'm nearly sick. This is just too important a decision to not spend a lot of thought on."

Finally at the end of her patience, Maude raised her voice so Harry definitely heard her. "Darn it Harry, you seem more interested in selecting a bull than thinking about the man your daughter is going to marry! Don't you even care about who may become your son-in-law?"

"Of course I care, but I just figured the bull

was more important. We'll get thirty calves from him every year. We'll need those calves to support this no-account she's marrying. Besides, we'll only get two or three offspring from him and hundreds from the bull."

Growing Up Weird

It has been pointed out that in order to write a monthly column you have to be strange. When that column is as strange as "Under The Wire", it is a dead give away that the author not only marches to the beat of a different drummer but he is marching the other direction as well.

The facts are, my kids are right, I guess I am strange. I look at things a little differently than some, I suppose.

It all started when I was a kid. I had an unusual childhood. Other kids my age wanted to grow up to be race car drivers, football players or maybe doctors. I wanted to be a cowboy. (Except for playing doctor in the 2nd grade with a neighbor girl who made medicine more interesting!)

Since we hadn't heard of astronauts yet, most kid's heroes were movie actors or stars on the new fangled TV sets everyone was getting about then.

My heroes were cowboys. A lot of kids idolized cowboys then but even at that I was different. The others longed for an autograph from Roy Rogers, Gene Autrey or the Cisco Kid. Not me. Few had even heard of my heroes.

When I talked of my heroes: Casey Tibbs, Jim Shoulders or Toots Mansfield, nobody had ever heard of them. That tends to warp a child when nobody knows who your heroes are.

I'd just as well have said they were Deb Copenhaver, Walt Linderman or Todd Watley for all the good it would have done. The other kids wouldn't have known them either (they, too, secretly were on my hero list). These were all real cowboys.

They didn't wear fringed shirts or ride silver-mounted saddles. They ate dust, rode broncs with ease and roped calves with a grace I could only dream about.

Never the less, it affected me. When other kids were playing cowboys and Indians, I wanted to play "cowboys in pickups" going down the road to the next rodeo.

When other kids talked about the Lone Ranger's horse, Silver, I wanted to talk about Baby-Doll, the best bull doggin' horse in the country.

Other kids just sort of looked at me like I'd come from another planet. It had to effect me.

On aptitude tests administered in grade school, I was asked to mark what I wanted to do if I was allowed to grow up. There were boxes to mark fireman, dentist, teacher and other conventional occupations. I always wrote "cowboy" across the bottom. That got me lots of sessions with the school counselor, nowadays called a "shrink".

I couldn't help it, I wanted to make my living wearing boots and a hat. It's all I ever wanted to do. I was strange.

I don't know what ever happened to that grade school "counselor" or most of the kids who marked dentist on their aptitude test.

I do know that at the moment I'm writing this I'm wearing boots and there's a cowboy hat hanging by the door. When I finish, there's a horse standing outside for me to go rope on. They were right, I probably was (and am weird), but I'm living my dream. How are they doing?

The Milk Cow Blues

I'm in the cattle business. That means I buy, sell, own, or otherwise care for bovines. Over the years I've probably owned about every kind of cow critter known to man. In the years to come, I'll own more of every kind for a few days, weeks or months...

Except one.

I will never, ever, not even for a minute own the meanest, most hateful, troublesome creature alive. I'm not talking about a Brahma bull, a Longhorn cow or even a thoroughly upset Hereford. That most creatively evil animal I'm referring to is a family milk cow.

I'm not condemning milk cows in general. A lot of my good friends make their living off a set of productive commercial dairy cattle. The creature I'm talking about is the old gentle, "nurse maid to a nation" family cow.

I'm sorry, I don't like 'em, never have. My father had them and I hated them (really it was them who seemed to hate me). I owned a few in my adult life and they, too, hated me. No other animal can eat and drink all day out in the corral and never go to the bathroom until they get inside the milk barn.

No other creature could stand by docilely while you fill your milk bucket and at the last possible moment swing her tail in such a way as to deposit a little used hay and corn into the milk bucket.

The family milk cow is the only critter I've seen who can walk into the same barn and put her head into the same stantion day after day for months. The one day you are in a hurry to leave and have about five minutes to milk, she suddenly forgets everything she ever knew about entering barns. Her face shows she has forgotten the concept of putting her head into the stantion. After you rope her and drag her into the proper place, she proceeds to put her foot into the bucket of milk (what little she gave), while swatting you up alongside your head with her tail.

Accidents you say? No siree. The actions of a scheming diabolical mind.

My "favorite" milk cow was a small Holstein cross I had years ago. As a first calf heifer she was ideal. She raised her calf plus everything else I put in with her. When I needed milk for the house, I only had to shut the calves up in the morning and that night she gave me an easy bucket of milk. The next year I was ready when she calved. I had three baby calves ready to put on her to raise. This old gal was going to help lift the mortgage this year.

I was set up.

When she calved she wouldn't take my purchased calves. She wouldn't take her own calf either. What's more, she wouldn't put her head in the stantion she had looked forward to entering twice a day last year. One "training session" ended with all four feet tied up and her laying on the milk room floor. Needless to say, we went to 7-11 for milk that night. The end result was I had to buy milk replacer for four bottle calves and feed an unproductive, dry, small Holstein cow all winter. (I couldn't sell her, I owed the bank more on her than she would have brought.)

Someone said just today how high milk was in the stores right now. I say it's cheap at twice the price. The local grocery store can count me as a good customer for the rest of my life!!

VAG
STEVE ALLER
96

A Horse is a Horse, of Course

All cowboys and cowgirls recognize there is a special attachment between a rodeo contestant and their horse.

Some, mostly the ladies, get all gooey eyed when they talk about their favorite horse. The attachment barrel racers have for a big hearted, winning mount, borders on fanatical. These horses get treatment and affection a cowboy can only dream about receiving from the ladies.

The guys, on the other hand, vary in the way they show appreciation for a favorite horse. They may just mumble, "I guess he's O.K.," when asked about their steed, then give him a little pat when they think no one is looking. If the horse happens to be for sale, however, then they too may get quite affectionate and utter words like, "Yep, he's probably the best son-of-a gun I've ever owned. In fact, it just might be he's the best anyone's ever owned!" Their true affection more than likely though will be a few extra brush strokes or checking his water bucket one last time before retiring to the camper for the night.

All this is leading up to a chance for me to relate a story about a cowboy and his horse and a truly memorable ocurrance I observed a couple of years ago...

I was attending a calf roping jackpot during the winter months at a town near by. About halfway thru the second go-around, Sam (not his real name because he may not think this story is as funny as I do) roped a calf, stepped off and went down the rope. The old sorrel horse really got in the ground on his stop, took about two steps backward and promptly fell over dead. If you had set up a fiberglass statue of a horse in his position, then pushed it over on it's side, it wouldn't have fallen cleaner and laid more still.

After a few stunned moments, we all ran out to help. Knives flashed and Sams rope was immediately cut into about seven pieces. In fact, I haven't seen that many knives appear so quick since I accidently walked into a biker bar a few years ago and said, "Damn it smells funny in here!" That is another story.

Anyway, old sorrel's saddle and bridle were pulled off quickly and someone tried a form of

CPR on him by jumping up and down on his belly in his boots and spurs. If I'm ever injured at a rodeo, I sure hope that guy is nowhere near as I lay on the ground. As we all stood around the very dead calf horse, I discovered I was standing next to a very depressed looking Sam, the owner of the horse. I felt I should offer some words of condolence, "Well, Sam," I said, "At least old Sorrely died doing something he loved."

Sam turned, looked at me and in the tenderest tone he was capable of, uttered the epitaph that will live in my mind forever.

"The son-of-a-#*&!#@ never liked this anyway. Someone call the rendering truck."

A Little Sugar Makes the Medicine Go Down

I received a phone call from the feedlot today. It wasn't good news, a heifer I had on feed there had died.

Now, for a cattleman that news isn't really news. "The only guy who don't have trouble with cattle don't own any," an old neighbor told me once.

Even though this wasn't an unusual call, it got me to thinking. It had to be hard for the feedlot manager to make that call. His promises of three pounds per day gain and eighty percent grading choice in one hundred twenty days kind of withered. The call certainly wasn't easy on me either. The promise I'd made to the bank to give them their money back sort of faded, also.

What this feedlot needs to do is study the

evening news. The anchor man and weather man laugh and joke while telling of wars, earthquakes and crashes. The idea, I suppose, is to relieve some of the tension the seriousness of the news creates.

Why couldn't the feedlot use the same tactics? Why not mail me a cute little note with a few bright cheery lines to ease the shock of the message...

Hurray, Hurray,
Your heifer died today.
No more feed bills to pay.
She just walked in and looked around,
Walked over to the corner and crashed to the ground.
Just one problem still is left,
A reminder of her untimely death.
She's now turned into food for a pet,
But the scavengers haven't paid us yet.
When they do, we'll mail it, no doubt,
After taking her feed bill out.

The monthly feed bill, now a source of anguish, could also be lightened up....

Roses are red, violets are blue,
Once again your monthly feed bill's due.
Our yardage is up, corn is too,
So we're happily passing these costs on to you.

Please pay by the tenth, or better yet,
Send it now, prompt payment's a good bet.
Cause cattle may die, or the market go down,
We don't want to be looking for you all over town.
So pay real quick, please don't delay,
Interest won't go down, but the market may.

Finally the packer could send you a light-hearted message after they kill your cattle grade and yield. Along with the report could come a note like this:

Well, Mr. Feeder, your cattle are all dead,
You expected $114 but we're giving you $84 instead.
Some were too fat, others too lean,
Some just were the wrong color, see what we mean?
We deducted the shrink, killing charges, too,
The rest we've kindly sent on to you.
It may not seem like much, we agree.
But we're glad you didn't sell them to IBP.
We need the profit your cattle generate,
So next Monday morning our buyer'll be at your gate.
Sell us some more, we need them bad,
You're one of the easiest we've ever had!

I'm sure you all agree these little notes would sure make you look forward to those boring trips to the mailbox.

The Hodgson Factor

If I remember correctly from my old textbooks, it takes about eight pounds of feed to convert to one pound of beef. For one pound of pork it takes about four to five pounds of feed. A chicken does better at about two pounds of feed to make a pound of drumstick.

I understand that fish can convert almost one to one, which has to have been the record. I say it has to have been in the past because I believe I've found a new record holder.

"What kind of animal is more efficient than the above mentioned animals?" you ask.

Me. That's right, you're looking at the new world's record holder for conversion ratios. I only recently discovered that I had this talent.

Having reached the age that starts with a four sometime ago, I started to notice changes in the world around me. Thirty-three inch waist jeans no longer were as large as they used to be. The well-worn marks on my leather belt started to show up before they got to my belt buckle.

At first I placed these occurrences along with other unexplainable phenomena like the Bermuda Triangle, UFO's and Murphy's Law.

Then others started to make comments like my wife's, "I think we should buy your shirts a little larger next time," or my mother's, "Haven't you gained a little?"

My kids have inherited my gift of tact. When one of them said, "Dad, you're fat," I took the subtle hint and decided it was time to do something about it.

That's right, I went on a diet. It has been salad, small portions of lean beef and not a heck of a lot else now for the past several weeks. That was when I learned of my amazing conversion abilities that put a feedlot steer to shame.

I found I can live on virtually nothing and not loose weight! I can eat about a pound of salad (which is around a half bushel) and gain a pound. Heck, I can eat nothing and gain half a pound!

My body is the most amazing perpetual motion machine ever. You don't even have to feed it and it keeps on maintaining itself. I think I will probably donate my body to science when I'm done with it. Most major universities having a good animal science department will want to study its amazing self-sufficiency.

If they can identify and harness my amazing powers, it would revolutionize the cattle industry! In the future we may see a cow that requires no winter feed. Actually, you'll never have to feed her at all. Just gather the calves once a year.

The "Hodgson Factor", as it may become known, will be applied to feedlots also. Just build the pens and put the cattle in. Add a small amount of feed and come back in a few weeks and load out your fat cattle.

I have no doubts this will revolutionize the entire livestock industry. I should become famous, even if it is posthumously.

In the meantime, this unusual talent is getting me nowhere.

The only benefit so far is that it's sure helping out on the grocery bill around the old ranch house!

STEVE ALLER
'96

A Small Answer

I dialed the telephone and waited hopefully for an answer. This guy and I had been missing each other for weeks. Either I was out when he called, or he was gone when I called. "Phone Tag" they call it.

Suddenly my heart jumped. The phone stopped ringing and the click on the other end indicated someone had answered. I was elated. Weeks of electronic pursuit was over. Success!!

"Hewwo?" the small voice barely made it across the long distance lines.

It was obvious one of the younger, quicker family members had out-raced the older, slower adults to the telephone.

"Hello, is your father there?" I asked.

"Nooo," the little voice answered.

"What about your mother? Is she there?" I pressed, my heart sinking.

"Nope, she's with my daddy down by the pump house."

"I see, well can I..."

"She said she would help him once more but if he got mad and used bad words she was comin' back to the house for the rest of her life."

I could see the picture but this was costing me money and I just wanted to talk to the man of the house. Before I could interrupt, she went on.

"Yesterday, daddy got mad and threw his tools in the ditch and called the motor a word I'm not allowed to say. Mommy got mad and said not to talk like that and daddy said more bad stuff. Mommy even said 'No-No' words then and..."

I finally interrupted, "Can I call him tonight?"

"You see mister, I'm just a little girl so it takes me a long time to explain stuff so that's why this will take some time for me to tell you your answer."

I could tell she knew she had a real problem case on the phone and would have to be careful how she tried to explain stuff to me.

"Tonight we've got to go to Shirley's ball game in town. It starts at 7:00 and lasts until Suzy falls asleep."

"What time is that?" I shouldn't have asked.

"Well, she's just little and some days she's cranky and doesn't want to sit still. Then mommy gets mad at me for poking her."

I was losing control of this situation. "Could I call in the morning?"

"Uh...Yep that would be good, but don't do it when we're out doing chores. I've got a new puppy and he follows me everywhere I go."

This was getting expensive, but you just can't interrupt a good puppy story. Finally I got a break, "Could you tell your daddy Gary Hodgson called."

"Yep."

"Can you remember that?"

"Yep."

"Who are you going to tell him called?"

"You."

"What's my name?"

"I dunno."

"Gary Hodgson."

"Ok, bye."

Click.

The Interview

The young lady reporter met the cowboy at the cafe just as they had agreed.

"I'm so happy you are going to let me follow you around for a few days as background for the story I'm doing on rodeo cowboys," she said as they sipped their coffee. "This will fit in perfectly with stories I've already done on professional football, baseball and tennis players. Tell me," she continued, "how were you selected to be my host?"

"Well, Ma'am, we had a drawing at the last rodeo. Everyone's name was put into a hat."

"How exciting! Just the thought of all those cowboys standing around in excited anticipation of being selected! I'll bet you were thrilled to be the winner."

"No Ma'am," cowboy answered.

"No? You mean you weren't excited?"

"No, I mean I wasn't the winner," cowboy continued a little embarrassed. "They drew out all the names until only one was left, he got the job. My name got stuck under the sweat band and was the only one left. I tried to get them to draw again but one of the judges had done the drawing and everyone knows judges won't admit to making a mistake."

A little flustered the lady reporter muttered as she wrote, "Subject selected in a suspense-filled random lottery."

"Before we bang the road, as you cowboys say, let me ask ... "

"Hit the trail, Ma'am, not bang the road," cowboy corrected.

"That doesn't sound as sexual but ok, hit the road," she replied, "now tell me who's your coach?"

"Well, nobody and everybody," cowboy explained. "You see, cowboys aren't on teams with coaches, after college anyway, so really your only coaches are the other guys you're competing against."

"You mean you take the advice of people who are trying to beat you?" The astonished lady asked. "Who congratulates you if you beat them?"

"They do," cowboy answered.

STEVE ALLER
96

"Yea, right", the skeptical reporter said, shaking her head. "Who pays you?" she went on.

"Mostly the other contestants, I guess, except for a little money the rodeo committees put up," cowboy replied thoughtfully.

"You mean the other participants help you win, then pay you if you do?" she asked incredulously.

"I guess that sort of sums it up, Ma'am," cowboy responded.

"Look, fellow," the lady bristled, "If you're not going to be honest with me, I'm going to have to terminate this interview. I'm going to ask you one more question and your answer had better make sense or I'm leaving. Now, how much do they pay you to enter a rodeo and risk injury or death? This answer had better make sense to me!"

Cowboy stood up, tipped his hat and replied, "So long, Ma'am. If you didn't believe my other answers, you sure ain't going to like this one!"

An Unhealthy Situation

The three tired cowboys checked into the motel looking forward to a good night's sleep. This would be the first real bed they had seen for several days, having made seven rodeos in five days. Tonight there would be no naps in the car seat while someone else drove, no stops at 7 - 11 after midnight for gas and coffee and no cramped knees from sleeping in the car on the go. Tonight there would be sheets, a pillow and quiet.

No sooner had the three hit the mattresses when they were startled by a horrible noise in the next room. It sounded like someone had turned on five radios, all playing a different station, all at their loudest.

"Quiet down," the cowboy closest to the wall yelled thru the plaster as he banged on the wall by his bed.

He was answered with a blast of noise even louder than the first.

"Guess they didn't hear me," he said. Following a brief odd-man loses coin toss, one cowboy was elected to journey next door. When he knocked on the neighboring motel door, he was greeted by a big burley young man with, of all things, a saxophone dangling from his neck.

"Think you could hold it down a little in there? We're trying to sleep next door," the cowboy asked as he viewed four more men in the room sporting various musical instruments.

"Hell no we won't," the saxophonist glared. "We rented this room for our band to practice in and that's what we intend to do."

"Couldn't you just wait a few hours or something?" the frustrated cowboy queried.

The burley musician placed his saxophone in his mouth, blew a loud blast and slammed the door in the bewildered cowboy's face.

By the time the cowboy delegate had returned to his room, it was obvious his mission had been a failure. The room fairly shook as he explained his encounter with the Lawrence Welk from Hell.

"Come on, boys," one of the other cowboys said as he headed out the door, the other two right behind him.

Their knock on the door once again was answered by the sax-man, this time flanked by four others.

"I'm getting real tired of you goat-ropers interrupting our band session," sax-man glared.

"Sir, I believe one of these rooms is going to be empty tonight and I think it is going to be yours," the lead cowboy answered just in time to have all five musicians swarm out of the room, fists flying.

Before you could say Guy Lombardo, it looked like a hockey game there in the parking lot. It did not take three irritable cowboys long to dispatch five band members.

Just as the last musician hit the asphalt, a squad car rolled into the parking lot.

"We got a report from the motel manager of a group making too much noise in one of the rooms," the first officer out of the car remarked, "What's going on here?"

"Well, sir" the first cowboy grinned, "It was kind of a health education matter here. We just were teaching these boys to practice safe sax! Goodnight, officer."

The Hat

In order to understand this story you must wear a hat. I don't mean you have to go put a hat on to read it. I mean you have to be a regular wearer of the cowman and cowboy's trademark, the hat.

The people I'm talking to today are those who consider themselves to be naked unless they have their hat on.

These people will understand that your hat is your personality. You are what you wear. Your hat establishes to yourself and to others who you are.

Most of us hat wearers are very choosey about our hats. They've got to be shaped just so and placed just right on your head. I think I've got a notch in my skull where my hat sits, and it's only comfortable there.

Most of us have several hats. First, you have

your work hat. It'll be dirty, stained and maybe a little bent, but even then it has to be just right. It can get pretty unsanitary but don't you dare change a thing. When you put it on, your mind clicks into the work cycle. You're ready.

Second, we all have our "good" hat. This one is for "struttin". It really tells the world who you are or want to be, anyway. An experienced hat wearer can read you by the hat you wear. He can tell if you're a 'real hand' or 'not too handy'. He can even tell your financial status by looking at your hat. An experienced hat wearer can pick out a $250.00 unit in a second but how it's shaped and worn tells the tale.

"Real men don't eat quiche" and "real cowboys don't wear feathers". I'm not really sure what quiche is, but I know most cowmen wouldn't be caught dead with the rear end of a pheasant glued to the front of their Stetson or Resistol. However, once in a while you'll see a single big hawk or eagle feather drooping off the back of a 'real' hat. This part of the story is kinda off the track but it seemed necessary to mention anyway.

What I want to address is the psychological problem that hits us hat wearers twice a year. That problem is the switch from felt to straw in the spring and back to felt in the fall. We bonafide hat wearers suffer serious psychological changes.

After a winter of putting on old felt every morning you finally decide it's time to break out the straw. (We used to just go buy one; now they're so expensive we keep 'em for years of re-use.)

When you walk out of the house that first day with the straw on you feel silly. It ain't you! You just know everyone is looking at you and thinking, "Golly, he looks silly." Even your shadow looks funny! It causes real personality changes in a person.

Then, just when your straw becomes a part of you, we'll start having some cool mornings and it'll be time to switch back to the funny feeling felt. Once again you loose your identity for a week or two.

I'm telling you , it's a major problem only a serious hat wearer can understand.

There are several solutions besides psychiatric counseling. Some avoid the problem by never switching. They choose a felt or a straw and wear it year-round. I'll refrain from any observations on felts in July and straws in February.

Others, however, unable to handle the severe mental disorders that can arise have avoided the entire issue by wearing a cap.

I suppose they have a point. A cap is cheap (generally free). It doesn't blow off and some have earflaps. I guess you can wear one year-round if you want to.

For me, though, it just creates a mini-identity crisis. I just don't feel like me in a cap and my shadow really looks funny then!

Kiss My Keyboard

Over the years I have found many reasons I like horses and the horse business. Horses give me pleasure, fulfilment, etc., etc. Recently I've discovered still another reason I like horses. They'll never be computerized!

Every other facet of my life seems to be controlled by some sort of computer, lately. My car, my phone bill, my dental records, even entering a rodeo involves a computer somewhere along the line. These days when you enter a rodeo all the pertinent data, events to be entered, preferences, partners, is mixed with inputs such as perfs, slack, priorities. The mix is run thru the mechanical brain.

Thousands of possible combinations are considered before the conclusion pops up on the screen. You got drawn out.

While computer geniuses have figured out

how to make themselves indispensable to the world by attaching a computer to almost everything, no one has figured out how to computerize a horse. I love 'em for that.

The reason that all these Einsteins haven't been able to hook a computer up to a horse is simple. Computers use "logic" and a horse has no logic. Horses chose the most inappropriate times and places to forget everything they ever knew. Ever drawn the best bucking horse in the string only to have him walk out of the chute and say "hello" in horse talk to the pickup man's horse?

Calf ropers, have you ever had old Dobbin work perfectly at home, only to go to a rodeo and have him decide to walk up and see just what it is you do when you tie a calf?

Oh, sure, to computerize a horse would involve other problems. Like, where do you mount the keyboard and how do you keep him from chewing on the monitor? Cable length would be a problem on some, also. Especially on race horses going over 400 yards.

In short, I can see hundreds of problems associated with Radio Shack becoming your local tack shop. When you get on a horse, there's not a damn thing Apple or IBM can do about it.

Horses, I love 'em.

The Cure

The battered old pickup rolled into the yard of the new neighbors. It was always nice to stop by and let them know you were the next place down the road and friendly.

"Howdy," old Sam offered. "I'm Sam Jones, and I live next to you on the west. Just wanted to let you know I'm here to help if you need it."

"Well, gee," the fresh-faced newcomer beamed. "I'm Joe Smith and I'm sure glad to meet you. I'm going to need lots of help here because I don't have the faintest idea how to do this ranching thing."

"What are you doing here, then?" old Sam asked kind of puzzled.

"I was an accountant and my wife and I always wanted to live in the country. We finally decided to sell our practice in the city and move out here to ranch. Frankly, neither of us has ever done this type work before. I really do need some advice. Say, could you come over here to the barn with me a minute?"

"Sure," Sam volunteered. As they walked across the yard Sam notice the green-horn was limping.

"Hurt yourself?" Sam asked.

"Oh, no, it's just these new cowboy boots. They're hurting my feet."

"Let me see them a minute," Sam offered. When Joe had taken the crisp new boots off and handed them to him, Sam walked over to the stock tank and tossed them in.

"There, now put 'em on and wear 'em until they're dry. That'll fix 'em up fine."

"Boy, now if I could just get these new jeans to fit right, I'd be in good shape," Joe said.

"That's easy," Sam offered. "Just throw 'em in the tank like your boots, put 'em on and wear 'em until they're dry."

"Interesting," Joe observed. "What I want to show you is this new saddle I just bought. The stirrups are stiff and it hurts me everywhere I sit. What can I do?"

"Just watch," Sam said as he walked over and picked up the new saddle. He took it to the same stock tank and threw it in.

"Now put it on your horse and ride it until it's

dry and it'll never squeak or rub you raw again."

"Boy, that stock tank sure can fix a lot of things around here. I wish my wife was feeling better so she could see this. She either strained or broke her foot last night. We don't know what to do. She's up at the house right now. We're not certain whether it needs attention or not."

"Maybe I'd better take a look at it," Sam offered again. "I've seen lots of broken bones around these parts."

"Oh, no, we'd better not do that," the wide-eyed newcomer warned.

"Well, why not?" a startled Sam asked.

"You seem to have the same treatment for everything around here and she can't swim."

STEVE ALLER
96

The "Chore" of Hittin' the Road

For an awful lot of us cowboys and cowgirls the day starts off with "chores". Before anything else gets done or breakfast eaten, the stock must be fed.

Unless you live on a larger ranch, farm, or feedlot, chores generally don't amount to much, just throw old Brown some hay and water the ropin' stock. You hardly even think about it as you go thru the routine.

One day, though, you decide to hit the rodeo trail and suddenly chores get to be a big deal. The first problem is who to get to do them. You take a mental inventory of who you could impose on. Neighbors are the logical choices. Friends you've chored for during their vacations rank high also. Everyone who has morning chores becomes a member of an exclusive group I call the "hay-in-your-shorts-club". You see, each morning during chores you always manage to get a little hay down your neck. During the day, gravity goes to work and some time that morning the hay leaves get as far down as they can go. This is usually your Fruit of the Looms. There they remain all day to remind you of chores to be done that night again. People who work in town can especially appreciate the difficulty of conducting yourself with dignity while having your britches full of scratchy alfalfa hay leaves.

After making your selection and inviting your helper by to show them the process, the real trouble starts.

Suddenly your little insignificant chores you hardly thought about become huge tasks. You just kind of dabbled a little here, threw a little hay there and it worked. You have a system, yet you'll be darned if you can explain it to anyone. Typical instructions go like this:

"There's two horses in this corral. They don't get along when they eat so you've got to put the feed out separately. You can feed the sorrel in the shed and the bay outside. Now if the bay goes into the shed first, then you better close the gate on him because the sorrel will come in and they'll fight. You can let him out after you feed the kid's rabbits. You can water them from the hydrant over by the sheep pen. Oh, yea, I forgot about the sheep. Give them the rest of the bale left after you hay the horses. I just kind of grab a little off the end of the bale for them."

By then you are embarrassed and confused trying to explain your system (because you don't really seem to have a system). You decide not to even mention shaking a little grain out to the lame calf, turned out in the pasture by the house, if he comes in while you're feeding - but don't put it out if the grey horse comes in with him. If he eats the grain he'll get to feeling too good and buck you off when you get home.

We, of course, haven't even touched on the subject of the wife's house plants, the kid's cats and the fish in the aquarium, all of whom need attention.

Yep, it's tough being on the rodeo road, but it's even tougher gettin ready to go!

STEVE ALLER
96

The Country System

There is a movement across the country to change the way we measure, weigh and calculate things. It seems that the American way of using acres, gallons, inches, pounds, and such is too confusing to the rest of the world. All the other guys, you see, are using hectares, meters, liters and grams to figure things out.

I suppose this is kind of confusing to most people, but to some of us it's no big deal. If you live on a farm or a ranch or around livestock, you're already familiar with having a different system to weigh and measure.

For years livestock people have used a system of weights and measures different from the American or the metric system. For lack of a better name I'll call it the "Country System".

I have used the "Country System" for years. Most of you have too, you just didn't know it.

Right here in the heart of America we developed our own unique set of measurements.

Our system is based on several different units. First is the gallon. No, not the gallon you know based on four quarts. Our gallon is based on a three pound coffee can. These usually red containers are the basis for our volume measurement in the "Country System". They don't hold a traditional gallon but the coffee can is our standard unit of measurement. When anyone feeds a gallon of grain to their horse, you can bet it's a three pound coffee can full.

Now the problems start. The next measurement is five gallons (used by people with pigs or lots of horses) .... but there are six three pound coffee cans in a five gallon bucket.

Then there's our standard unit of weight measurement... the flake. This is a portion of a bale of hay universally recognized in the "Country System". The number of flakes in a bale vary according to the machinery used to bale it, moisture content and other factors. However, describe feeding the bucket calves in flakes of hay and anyone from the country will understand. This unit has been rather confusing lately with the advent of the big one ton hay bales!

Finally, our area measurement is the ground needed to run one cow on pasture. Called the cow unit, ranches sell by it, pastures get rented, evaluated and traded based on it. A cow unit, however, can vary from less than one acre on a farm in Greeley, Colorado to about 160 acres in parts of Utah.

I hope the National Bureau of Standards, the people who standardize our weights and measures, have preserved a three pound Folgers coffee can, a flake of North Park grass hay and a cow unit in Roswell, New Mexico. There is an entire industry who considers these units to be internationally understood. Keep your grams and centimeters, just go throw my horse two flakes of hay and half a gallon of grain, please.

Easy Cuisine

Lots of money and time have been expended trying to convince the public to eat beef. I've recently discovered another darn good reason.

It's easier.

No, I don't mean it's easier to prepare, cook or serve. I mean it's just easier to eat beef. Let me explain.

Occasionally "short person" decides she has spent enough time in the ranch kitchen and it's time I took her out to eat. Since these events don't happen too often, we try to make them special. The other day when the subject of going out to eat came up I discovered a new reason to eat beef.

Like everyone else, the Hodgson household enjoys a little variety in our diet. Seafood, pizza or even just salads get a try once in a while.

The other day we decided to eat Chinese.

The food's not too bad (they use some beef), the atmosphere is different and it's relatively cheap.

My problems started after we'd arrived and been seated. Now, nobody around the whole place seemed to be able to speak English real well. That was OK since it sort of added to the atmosphere. I needed to find the 'facilities' and that's when I got into trouble.

"Excuse me, Miss, but where are your restrooms?" I asked the waitress.

"Ah, restrooms down hall. You must turn on right," she said.

I followed the hall and found the men's restroom at the end of the hall, not on the right as she had said. I walked into total darkness. Feeling around on the wall in the darkness I found no switch, so I returned to the waitress.

"It's dark in there, Senorita," I said, forgetting we weren't in Los Amigos Mexican restaurant.

"You must turn on right," she repeated.

"Honey, if I turn to the right I'll be in the broom closet, I ain't using no mop bucket!"

"No, no, you must turn on right," she said more emphatically.

I went and looked on the right into the broom closet. It was dark in there, but even the mop bucket was starting to look good.

I tried logic next with my waitress person. "Look, lady, it's dark in both those rooms. Now granted, I can do a lot of this project from memory, but I still need a hint as to which way to face."

"Please come with me," she finally said.

So off to the restroom my guide and I headed. I was hoping nobody had seen this. I was also hoping she would just head me the right way and then leave. I wasn't up to a coed bathroom even if it was part of the atmosphere.

She marched me to the door at the end of the hall, pushed open the door and pulled the string dangling there in the dark.

"See Mr., you must turn on the right."

The Market Report

According to my calendar from the local feed store we'll soon have a full moon. This will affect the ocean, planting times, plus cause a rash of murders, muggings and other anti-social behavior.

I have observed another phenomenon that has the same effect on people. This force makes sane men crazy or vice-versa. Even weirder is that this can happen any Monday through Friday!

What is this force that can shape people's lives and change their destinies? "The Market Report."

No other single event can make or break your day like the market report. Just picture this in your mind. Father gets up in the morning and sits down to his morning cup of coffee. Mother is busy getting breakfast and the kids are getting ready for school. The radio is on. Suddenly, there it is, the morning market report.

The scene is now set. Let's say for now that the report is good. Fats are up $2, dressed meat is up $4 and the local auction reports feeders were up $4 last Friday. Dad is a happy man. He kisses his wife as he leaves the house after a wonderful breakfast. He takes time to ruffle the kids hair and even pats the dog as he leaves. His net worth just went up. All is well in his world.

Now look at scene two. The same setting with the same people, but the report is bad. Not just lower, but down, the report is bad, awful.

Dad is a changed man. Breakfast tastes like mud, he yells at his wife and ignores the kids. The dog hides behind the couch. It doesn't seem to matter that he really doesn't have anything to sell right now. The market is DOWN. The sun may shine that day, but he won't see it.

The market report gives us all a chance to do a mental financial statement each day. Most of us only sell a few times per year, yet the report is a must every day.

I shudder to think how many dogs get kicked because of a lower market. On the other hand, how many little pecks on the cheek are given when there's a good report?

I suppose we should be happy that the markets are only reported on weekdays, with little or no market activity on Saturday and Sunday.

That gives the wife and kids a chance to breathe easy and the dog can come out from behind the couch!

Cow Sense

Rural America used to be full of rural Americans. Now, that's not necessarily so.

The pristine lifestyle we in the country have enjoyed for generations has attracted others who wish to breathe the clean air of rural America. People who have lived in our cities are moving to the country. This not only helps out land values but also provides entertainment for the "old timers" of the area.

Things most of us sort of take for granted if we've lived in the area for years, come a little hard for these people.

A new "rancher" who had just purchased five acres of rocky hillside once asked, "How many cows can I run on my place?"

It was rather hard to explain that his spread would run 1/4 cow per year. This, of course, was if he sold his three horses.

When these new cowboys do get into the cattle business, it is a thrill a minute for everyone else, also.

At the local auction, the lady burst into the office," I want to see the manager at once!" she demanded. "Sir, I want to know why you gave my cow away for only 59 cents a pound. That came to only seven hundred thirty-seven dollars," the indignant lady went on.

"Excuse me, ma'am, but that is a darn good price for an open cow with one eye going bad," the manager pointed out.

"That shows how little you know!" the lady exploded. "That was a registered cow that only one year ago we gave $1,200.00 for. I know the market is higher, so she should be worth even more now!"

"Lady, it's November and your cow ain't bred. She's only worth weigh price now. She would have brought more if she had been bred, you know," the well-meaning auction man tried to explain.

"We sold her so we could buy a bull, Mister, but if you knew anything about cattle you would have known you were absolutely giving her away. I just can't believe you know so little about the cattle business!" she added.

"I guess you must be right, ma'am, because I

sure didn't know she was worth that much. But tell me, you seem to know an awful lot about the cattle business. Where did you learn about it?" the auction operator questioned.

"I've read four books on the subject plus the man who sold me that cow taught me a lot," she answered.

"I guess he sure did," the man replied, scratching his head.

Rise and Shine

Old bronc riders compare broken bones. Soldiers compare shrapnel scars. Football players compete for who took the worst hit or had the most knee operations. It's a "badge of courage" who can take the most pain.

Ranchers and farmers have their own way of comparing pain tolerance. Like all the other groups previously mentioned, their comparisons are unique to that group.

"What time do you get up?"

Ranchers and farmers take some sort of pleasure in getting up early. It's a "badge of courage" to get up before the sun.

Before the chickens.

Before everyone else.

Before good sense.

I know all about the pristine quietness of the world before the sun comes up. I know all about the calmness that sets over the world at 5:30 a.m. I should know, I have a father who has been working on the world record for continuously getting up early. His record right now, I believe, stands at seventy some years of being up before 5:30 a.m.

I realize that for many people the day just isn't long enough to get all their work done so they must start early.

I know dairymen must keep their cows on schedule. I also know a cow gives milk at 8:30 as well as 4:30.

The thing is, there is sort of a pride taken in getting up at a horrible hour. Oh, most don't come right out and say it. That would be bragging. Instead, they try to slip it into conversation. Lets say the conversation is about the weather. You will hear...

"It was zero when I got up this morning at four."

If you overhear guys talking about calving, pretty soon someone will say," I found this heifer calving down by the creek around 4:30 when I went out to do chores."

Granted, there are advantages of getting up with or before the sun. There's not much traffic on the roads. Generally, it's just you and few all night truck drivers.

The telephone party line usually isn't busy at 4:00 a.m. But you've got to be careful who you call at that hour!

I guess you can get a parking place just about anyplace in town about then, but, who cares?

Now, I know you're all wondering what about me. Am I one of those early risers? Well, just call me and we'll discuss it, but don't call before 8:00 a.m. or you'll get a busy signal. I take the phone off the hook so my father can't call to see if I'm up yet!!

The Cowboy Way

I have a few (not many, however) non-cowboy friends. If I were to list twenty of my closest acquaintances, fifteen would be cowboys. In my attempt to be a somewhat well-rounded person, I do associate with some "natives".

I hang around these people because their lifestyles and points of view intrigue me and I suppose mine is of interest to them.

The success of a recent movie, "The Cowboy Way", made me think that there must be a lot of people out there who wonder about what being a cowboy is all about. I didn't see "The Cowboy Way" because for me, part of being a cowboy is not really having the time or money to pay four dollars for popcorn. If I've got that much time or money, I'll head to a rodeo or at least the practice pen.

The following are a few points I have decided

that might explain to a civilian what it is like to be a cowboy:

DISCLAIMER: Any similarity between yourself and what I am about to write is purely intentional!

Being a Cowboy means:

The vehicle you drive has more miles on it than just about anyone you know...except for other cowboys.

Two thousand dollars is way too much to pay for carpet, but eight thousand dollars is not too high for a horse.

Any job you take must have good benefits. Not retirement, health insurance or profit sharing, but rather the boss must let you off whenever there's a rodeo to go to.

You are on a first name basis with the emergency room staff, not only of your local hospital but several others in various states and...

You hold frequent flyer miles for ambulance rides.

You remember things that happened not by reference points such as, near Thanksgiving, or two weeks before Labor Day, but by placing dates with references like, "while Cheyenne was going on" or " two days after the finals".

You are not real sure the exact dates of your kid's birthdays or how you spent your anniversary, but can remember exactly how fast you were at

STEVE ALLEN
'96

Hugo last year and what color the calf was.

You always have a spare shirt hanging from a hook in your car or pickup.

When you have to call home, you must call directory assistance for your number yet you can recite, from memory, the telephone numbers for entry offices of six different rodeo associations.

When you die you do not want to be remembered as a good dentist, farmer or radio broadcaster. Instead, at your funeral, you want someone to say, "He was a good cowboy."

The Lowly Fly

Rural America is the birthplace of quaint sayings that explain much in very few words. Even before Will Rogers, the country philosopher has been famous for this straight forward cut-thru-the-bull wisdom. Occasionally, though, I have to wonder about the accuracy of a few of these sayings.

You may read this during the same cold weather I'm writing it in. It is colder than a banker's heart outside, yet here in my office I have been bothered all morning by a fly. In spite of weather that can kill a calf outside, inside a fly survives. For some reason the old expression, "Dying like flies," came to mind.

I believe this phase was meant to symbolize some type of gigantic die-off. If we, "died like flies", the quest for perpetual life might be found. I know I've swatted this same fly five times and he seems to bounce back to circle my head again and again.

Am I overreacting you ask? Consider this. Thousands, millions, perhaps even billions of dollars have been spent for years to eradicate the fly. How much have you alone spent on fly tags, spray and bait? I've probably spent a fortune on fly swatters. This doesn't even take into consideration countless newspapers turned into weapons only to be torn in half or to have key words blotched out after contact with a winged nuisance.

Yet, after all these efforts and expenses, does anyone notice any fewer flies around? Of course not, they thrive in the face of our assault. If conversation between flies could be intercepted, surely we would hear them laughing at our feeble efforts. Did I say feeble? Entire labs full of P.H.D's, highly paid and respected, work year around to develop toxins to rid the world of flies. O.K., maybe not the world, how about the state? The county? Well, then, what about something that will keep 'em off my horse more than five minutes?

On the other side of the battle, the loosely organized society of flies with no labs, scientists or even an annual convention seem to come up with a counter play to our every move.

We try to keep our human population thriving,

yet mankind is attacked by every conceivable threat to it's existence. Yet everything in the good chain from frogs to college professors have been killing flies for centuries. Who seems to be winning?

Dying like flies? Maybe we should be so lucky.

Something Stupid

It seems like whenever I do something stupid someone is always there to see me do it. Even worse, when I do something really stupid, my wife is there to see it.

You husbands out there have probably observed this before. The last person in the world you need to have observed a little error on your part is the "Mrs".

Now, my wife usually doesn't try to embarrass me by retelling the story. She's real good about not further humiliating me. I think it may be because she doesn't want anybody to know what a fool her husband can be. I suppose it would reflect poorly on her standing with other wives. I can just hear them over coffee, "Boy, that Sue sure bombed out when she picked that one! Did you hear what he did now?"

Regardless of whether she retells the story

or even mentions it at all, she knows. You know she knows. She can give you a little look that says, "I know." Along with that little look is also the unspoken threat, "I know and if you don't toe the line I'll use it against you." I never know when, where or even if she would use it, but that look says she might.

My latest indiscretion involved a little trip to the pasture the other day. It was hot, dusty and I was running short of time. Things had not been going real well and my disposition was getting a little "tender".

As we were bouncing along across the sagebrush in a pickup that really shouldn't have been out there being treated like that in the first place, my wife leaned over with an observation.

"Honey," she said politely, "your gas gauge is on empty."

"Don't worry, I've got another tank," I answered, feeling smug for being so well prepared.

"Shouldn't you switch tanks before you run out?" she inquired.

"I always let it run out before I switch over," I replied. Boy, women don't understand mechanical things at all!

"I think you really should switch before it runs out", my little mechanic side kick persisted.

Now pushed beyond the limits of my good

nature and frustrated by her lack of automotive knowledge I gently explained, "Look, I've driven this pickup seven thousand miles since we bought it this spring. I always let it run out before I switch tanks. It always works. Men know these things. Now drop it OK?" No sooner had I "lined her out" when old pickup gave a cough and drank the last drop of gas from the left tank. Casually I leaned over and punched the switch to convert to the right tank. You guessed it. Nothing. Pickup rolled to a stop. Casually, then frantically I pumped the gas pedal. Nothing! I ground on the starter. Nothing. I worked the switch back and forth as I ran the starter. Nothing. Panic. My manhood was at stake here. Silence. Silence from the pickup, anyway. Not from my wife, however. Sue was thinking it. I knew she was. She didn't say a word, but she was thinking it.

Hood up, temper flaring and flies biting I worked on my stalled transportation. Vapor locked, I had no gas in the lines.

After thirty minutes of crawling under and over the engine unhooking lines, including one brilliant idea I had that blew gas from the tank all over Sue, the pickup finally started.

On the drive home the silence was deafening. Finally, I couldn't stand it any longer. "I know what you're thinking," I shouted. "Something

STEVE ALLER
96

went wrong. It always worked before!"

"All you would have had to do was take my advice," she mentioned.

Things got ugly for a while after that, but as usual we got over it.

Only now SHE knows. I live under the constant fear she will tell the story at the worst possible time. She gives me that look and I start to cringe.

But, now you all know. She can't hold it over my head any longer. I guess I showed her, huh!

A Bargain

I was standing in the lobby of the local auction the other day when it happened. A man walked up to me and asked, "Excuse me, sir, but what kind of after shave do you wear?"

Talk about mixed emotions. I didn't know whether to punch this guy and run, just ignore him and slowly ease away, or actually answer him. If I had been walking down the streets of San Francisco the question might have seemed more appropriate, but hey, this was macho land, one of the last strongholds of masculinity, the local livestock auction.

As thousands of thoughts raced through my head, I looked this guy over. No earring and no sandals. He wasn't holding hands with another guy. In short, he looked normal. I thought of all the answers I could give him:

"My fragrance is Guernsey #5. My old milk

cow dabs a little behind each of my ears every morning when I milk."

Another possible answer was, "Thank you for asking. I created this fragrance myself. I call it yesterday's clothing. Tomorrow you will be able to notice without even having to stand next to me."

I also thought of saying, "Well, thank you, big boy. And I just love your blouse. Where in the world did you ever find it?"

Well, I didn't say any of those things. Instead, I turned to him and stammered, "I, I, I think it's ... Old Spice. Why?" (Pretty smart answer, huh?)

"Well, sir, I represent a company that handles closeouts on major products and I can offer you a special deal on Giorgio, Brute or Obsession." At least now I knew what the deal was. Another guy had been by yesterday selling day-old seafood. The day before that it had been wrench sets made in Taiwan and pecans from Georgia.

"I'm sorry, sir," I answered, "but my kids give it to me for Christmas and birthdays. I guess this last year I got about half a gallon of the stuff. Since some days I never get around to shaving at all, I suppose I've got a two year's supply right now."

"Well, how about the little lady at home?" he persisted. "I can let you have any name brand you want for fourteen dollars a quart. You just furnish the container."

Well, folks, I know a good deal when I see one. I've got my Christmas shopping done for Sue this year. I hope she doesn't mind the old fly spray bottle I had to put the stuff in.

You know, most of those guys that come around selling things are just looking for a sucker. I think I was really smart not to fall for the others and to recognize a real bargain when it came along.

The Auction

The gate opened and cattle milled into the auction ring.

"Well, all right sir, what'a ya goin' to give for 'em," chanted the auctioneer. "These are the Curley, Larry & Moe cattle from Too Far, Wyoming. These cattle have had..." At this point, he then begins to describe all the medicine and management practices that have created these good cattle.

He may just say, "They've had all their shots," or he may try to pronounce all the names of the vaccines the seller has copied off the bottles onto the piece of paper the auctioneer now holds in his hands.

According to the list of vaccines the seller has furnished, the calves must bring a dollar a pound just to pay the medicine bill. After listening to the long lists of shots every consignor has given it makes you want to rush out and purchase stock in a drug company. If all these shots were in fact given, you wonder how some of the cattle survived all the puncture wounds.

This is all done in the name of salesmanship and most of these shots were really given. If helps to let the potential buyers know the background of the cattle being offered for sale. This information is helpful so he can take the cattle home and plan his own vaccination program.

Just once, though, I'd like the auctioneer to read off the real background of the cattle. Some might sound like this: "All right, folks, these cattle have had everything. Not the shots, the diseases! They had scours as babies, pneumonia last spring, and a touch of red nose this fall. They got out on the hayfield and a lot of them bloated. Two got out on the road and were hit by the neighbor kid's pick-up. They healed up and I paid for the new grill on the pick-up."

"That one over there in the corner of the ring was the hired man's roping calf; he said it was the best one he ever had because it stayed the same size all summer."

I'd like to hear the auctioneer say, "Of course these cattle have had all their shots! They've had combiotic, terramycin, turkey medicine and Geritol. It took everything we could think of just to keep ‘em alive when we got ‘em in from Florida last spring. Take ‘em home and love them because we sure got attached to them with all the times we put them through the old squeeze chute.”

Heck, everybody has trouble with cattle from time to time. A friend told me once, “The only people that don’t have trouble with cattle don’t own any!”

I guess nobody wants to brag about what a good job they did of keepin’ ‘em alive. They want it to look easy so all the doctor and lawyer investors will want to come in and buy their good replacement heifers!

The Computer Ages

I must be getting old. I won't say just how old I am, but when I graduated from high school a '57 Chevy was eight years old. Once in a while, however, things happen that make me feel old. Old and out of touch. Lately this feeling is brought on by new technology. Computers have a way of pointing out I have missed the boat. I just don't comprehend the wonders of electronics. Kids understand computers, I don't.

Unfortunately, computers are everywhere. My kids get games for Christmas that have computers built into them. The latest game plugs into a T.V. set and challenges the kids to find "warp zones" past "killer turtles"! To me a "warp zone" is any place I nailed up green lumber on my ranch fences. I won't even get into the turtle thing. I can't even play with their toys anymore!

My car has an "on board computer". One

day as I was driving down the road sixty-five miles an hour, the computer told the spark plugs the car was in the garage at home. Wham, the plugs went silent and I had to walk home. Repairs? You've got to be kidding. You don't call for a mechanic, you call a programmer to fix your car. There was a time when I was able to fix my own car. I have every size of Crescent Wrench ever made, but now I have no use for them.

Telephones make me feel outdated, too. We have new phones in our offices. They chirp, squeal and perform dozens of cute tricks, all the result of a built in computer. Trying to learn to use these phones was something else. One feature is " hands-free calls". You don't even lift the receiver, you just talk.

I called my friend to try out my skills. The phone worked fine so I started to tell old Rusty a joke I'd just heard. I was sitting there at my desk, arms folded, talking proudly as my new speaker phone fed my words to Rusty. I looked up to see several people watching me sitting there talking to myself. Feeling they needed an explanation, I explained how the phone worked and that someone really was listening on the other end. " Say Hi, Rusty," I said. There was only silence coming from the speaker as the people started to back away. I yelled into the phone, "Rusty, you ~#^~#!, tell them you're there!" The people began shaking their heads as they edged further away. Finally, after everyone had left, a chuckle came across the speaker.

Maybe I am getting old. I long for the days when a chip came from buffalo. Whatever happened to simple kiddy toys? Give me the days of crank phones, not crank calls.

I'm just not cut out for the computer age.

A Real Clothes Horse

"Just where do you think you're going?"

"Well, I thought we were going to rope at the local rodeo, Honey." I answered back, rather puzzled at my wife's question.

"You're not going anywhere dressed like that!" a stern Sue ordered.

"What's wrong with these clothes? They were OK yesterday and just fine this morning. I don't see why they suddenly aren't OK now," I replied, still a little confused.

"You get in there and put on those new black jeans and I'll pick out a shirt to match," my four foot eleven fashion advisor ordered.

"Sue, I'm goin' to a rodeo not a fashion show. I wear these same kinda clothes everywhere else I go. Why not now?"

"This is your hometown and I'll not have you going out there looking like a bum of some kind!"

Now, I'm a little slow at times but even I could tell we were not having a discussion here. The issue had already been decided, so I had best shut up and go along with this decision. Besides, I had a plan. I'd go along with the clothes bit, but I would put my old boots on out by the back door and slip out before Sue saw me.

"And by the way, wise guy, don't try to get out of here in those old boots, either. You put on the other pair I set out for you," the voice added. Darn, I hate when that happens.

When we arrived at the rodeo I felt like I should be going to church, or at least be announced as a visitor from out of town attending his first rodeo ever.

As I saddled up I tried to get as much dust on those shiny boots as possible just to feel more at home. I may even have brushed the horses a little extra trying to create a little hair and dust to stick to those black Wranglers.

When I rode into the arena to rope my steer, I fully expected the announcer to say, "And now, looking very chic in his new black jeans and matching shirt, here's that roguish, best-dressed hometown boy out to dazzle you with a very subtle fashion statement. Oh, by the way, why don't you rope while you're out there."

He didn't, however, seem to notice my clothes

and neither did anyone else. I roped my steer and left the arena.

I'm sure Sue watched, feeling confident she had prepared me in the best possible manner for this contest.

I rode out smugly carrying my secret that under these fancy clothes I had worn my oldest underwear and had on socks that didn't match! A guy has to protect his image, you know.

The Boot Theory

Asking a man how many cattle he has is like asking someone what their net worth is or how much money they have in the bank. You just don't do it. If you should accidentally commit this blunder you put the cowman in the uncomfortable position of having to either ignore you or lie to you. It just ain't polite.

Still we all judge a cattleman's success by how many head he has. We all are curious about things like this, even though what should also be considered is to subtract out how much is owed before judging the man's worth in cattle.

"It's not what you have, but what you get to keep," is a saying that sums up the situation.

For those of you that still want to know all about a cattleman's holdings, I propose a fairly sure-fire system for you.

I call this the "boot system". To figure out

how many cattle a rancher has, look at his boots. Here are the guidelines to follow:

1. Shiny, clean boots preferably of some exotic leather indicate a man who has always wanted to own cattle, but doesn't yet.

2. Good boots, but pretty beat up indicating lack of care the last few months. This wearer probably has recently purchased a few cattle and found out you have to do most of the work yourself if you want it done right.

3. Scuffed, dry, cracking, generally worn-out boots show the man with a sizeable investment in cattle. He's too poor to buy a new pair, too far from town to get them fixed and just too tired to care how they look.

4. Want to find the man with lots of cattle? Look for no boots at all. Heavy lace-up Red Wings or other work shoes probably mark this guy. He's too busy to keep up the image. Besides, since the cowboy fad hit, he hasn't wanted to spend the money to look like a cowboy. He knows who he is and doesn't care if anyone else knows or not.

In short, look at the boots. The worse shape, the more cattle. No boots, probably more than the average holdings.

OK, you're probably wondering what group I'm in. Well, the truth is, there's one more group

I haven't told you about and I'm in that one. I'm wearing tennis shoes. Good old tenny-lamas. My group has been in the business long enough to owe everyone in town money. The tennis shoes help me out-run the banker and feed store owner when I see them on the street in town!

On the Road

I seem to spend a lot of time driving these days and I enjoy it. Since my vehicle has not gone "cellular", my time behind the wheel isolates me from the world for a few hours and I get time to think.

Actually that's when these stories are born. My mind gets to apply itself to topics that normally I wouldn't get to spend time on — weighty, important stuff like other vehicles on the road and why are they there?

When driving across Western Kansas the other day I passed a truck with a huge boat in tow. This boat had to have an ocean or at least a very big lake to float it. I asked myself, "Why is it in Kansas?" Kansas is a long way from an ocean. If a manufacturer was moving it, why didn't they just move their factory nearer the ocean? Did someone in Kansas order the boat? Won't they be disappointed to discover there is nowhere to float it? Why was it there?

I also passed a truck loaded with large flat rocks. That's all, just rocks. Now to a kid who was raised up to his post hole digger handles in rocks, it was inconceivable to me that anyone would have taken the time to haul rocks. A lot of Kansas has no rocks it appears. Is there a government relocation program to put rocks there, or is the reason there seems to be none because they hauled them all away?

The boredom of miles of Interstate makes rather insignificant things take on new importance. A tractor setting in a field in February makes me wonder, "Why is it there?" Obviously there's no farming taking place in February. Did an absent minded farmer forget to take it home last fall? Hasn't anyone missed it yet? Does he just want to be the first in the field this spring?

I like to read road signs during these times, also. One sign outside a town proclaims "1,000 happy people and one grouch!" The sign seems kinda old so I wondered — Is that still the ratio or has being around all those happy people helped the grouch to cheer up? Or if one rotten apple can spoil the barrel, should the sign now read 1,001 grouches?

I wonder as I pass billboards — do people really

stop just to see a five legged cow or the world's largest prairie dog? Signs proclaiming a town to be the home of someone famous interest me.

Do they take them down when that person gets so famous they move to L.A.?

Oh, well, on my next trip I will address the burning issue of why the mileage on the road signs never seems to add up correctly!

Position or Job?

Some people have jobs. Others have positions. It used to be everybody wanted a job. Now, everybody wants a position.

It seems like a job has certain bad connotations today. A job means a time clock, regular hours and, heaven forbid, a pair of gloves. A position, on the other hand, seems to infer prestige, clean fingernails and "doing lunch" with the client.

If you want to hire today, don't advertise for someone to do a job. Don't bother, no one will answer. Instead, advertise for someone to "fill a position". Your phone will ring.

The problem with all this is that in the cattle business, there aren't many "positions". There are, however, a lot of "jobs".

A possible solution to finding an employee might be to change the way we look at our "jobs".

It seems that the big difference is that a "position" has a title, while a "job" has none. Maybe we can jazz up "jobs" by giving them titles.

Here are a few titles to make jobs into positions:

Hydrology Management Engineer (irrigator)

Mechanical Power Source Manager (tractor driver)

Livestock Inventory Manager (feedlot pen rider)

Feedlot Health Manager (feedlot pen rider)

Livestock Waste Disposal Executive (manure truck driver)

Supervisor of Necrotic Bovines (rendering works truck driver)

Pasture Containment Specialist (fence builder)

You get the idea. Use a few big words to describe the "job" and bingo, you've now created a position.

Over the years I have had several "positions". I was once a Petroleum Distribution Manager (worked at a gas station). I held the position of Plant Emergence Control Officer (cultivated sugar beets) and Grounds Maintenance Supervisor (mowed the boss's lawn). I have also been a Volume Purchaser (bought books at a college bookstore). Actually, I have done most of the

STEVE ALLER
96

"jobs" listed earlier, with no titles attached.

Not everything is good about having a position. It seems that, along with "positions", come headaches. It seems that the most common positions I have held have been "Over the Barrel", "Under the Gun (or Wire)", "Neck on the Chopping Block" or the dreaded "Held Accountable".

I have titles like "Hey you!" or "Go'fer". You know, go fer this, go fer that.

Oh well, it could be worse. I could have to go get a job!

My Kingdom For A Horse

I love to rope and that requires a horse. Actually, I would enjoy rodeoing a lot more if it did not require a horse. (No, thank you, bull riders, that is not a solution, for me anyway.)

It seems to me that the more you ask a horse to do, the more unhappy a person you become. The happiest easy-goingest guys in rodeo seem to be the bull doggers. They walk into the arena minutes before they're up, get on somebody's horse and then immediately jump off him onto a completely unbroken steer. That tells you right away their feelings about horses. They roll in the dirt, get horned, stepped on and come up grinning. They are just so darn glad not to need a horse any longer than that.

Team ropers are next in line. They never get off but will risk fingers, even hands to only have to ride for five or six seconds. "I've got to ride you, but let's do it quickly, ok?"

The most neurotic male horsemen in rodeo are the calf ropers. (Put me in this list.) We rope, then get off and expect this animal to go ahead and do stuff to help us. " Yeah, right." The result is a constant search for the animal that is smarter than we are, yet still wants to work for us.

It's hard to out do barrel racers for sheer paranoid behavior. Probably no one in the horse world knows more about horses and takes better care of them than barrel racers. They, however, have to ride them longer in a performance than anyone else and it has an effect on their personalities. (I suppose the only worse condition would be a male barrel racer.)

We are all on a constant search for the ultimate horse. We try 'em, buy 'em, use 'em and sell 'em. You have a horse you don't like? Good, I'll buy him. Maybe he will be strong where I'm weak and we'll fit perfectly. We all dream of finding a winner working in a feedlot and having him make us rich and famous. In the meantime we create a booming business for auction operators, horse traders and, yes, psychiatrists and marriage counselors.

A friend of mine said his first wife ran off with the best horse he ever had. He sure misses that horse.

I've Been Everywhere

A song title goes, "I've been everywhere, Man, I've been everywhere." The singer goes on to list in rapid-fire succession the names of all the places he's claimed to have been.

Rodeo cowboys and cowgirls have one up on this singing geography expert. They not only can name the places they've been but also tell you when their rodeo is and how to get to the rodeo arena in each town.

This last skill, finding the arena, is a talent most rodeo contestants take for granted, yet I'm sure the world would find remarkable. Just think about it. A contestant visits a town one time, moves on and doesn't return for perhaps several years, yet tucked away in their head is an exact road map leading them to the rodeo grounds. Not only can they find them personally, they also can give everyone else directions.

I know in some towns finding the fairgrounds isn't so tough. The grandstands may be the tallest structure in town, or there in fact, may hardly be a town.

You don't really have to be a rocket scientist to find the arena in Akron, Colorado; Torrington, Wyoming; or Sutherland, Nebraska.

Other towns aren't quite so easy. Billings, Montana is large enough to conceal a pretty fair sized rodeo arena. So is Dodge City, Kansas, and Agoura Hills, California. Yet, just about any contestant who was ever there one time can tell you how to find the "pens". Evidently, built into the brain of anyone bitten by the rodeo bug is a sort-of homing device that is attracted to dust, hot dog stands, rosin, horse hair and bull manure.

I'm really not sure why this phenonenam exists. Maybe having old number 14 slam dunk you makes the visit memorable. Perhaps getting a check at a rodeo forever carves a notch into your brain. It could be that we all just want to remember the places we spend some of the best moments of our lives. I'm not sure how it works but you will agree, it does.

Probably the thing I find the most amazing about the whole process is this — the same people who can direct you to the fairgrounds in hundreds of towns, in a dozen states, still have trouble remembering things like where are the car keys, how long do you set the microwave to ‘nuke’ a frozen burrito, and their wife (or husband’s) birthday?

I can’t remember where the dry cleaners are in Brush, but if anyone needs to know where the arena in Silverthorne is, just give me a call.

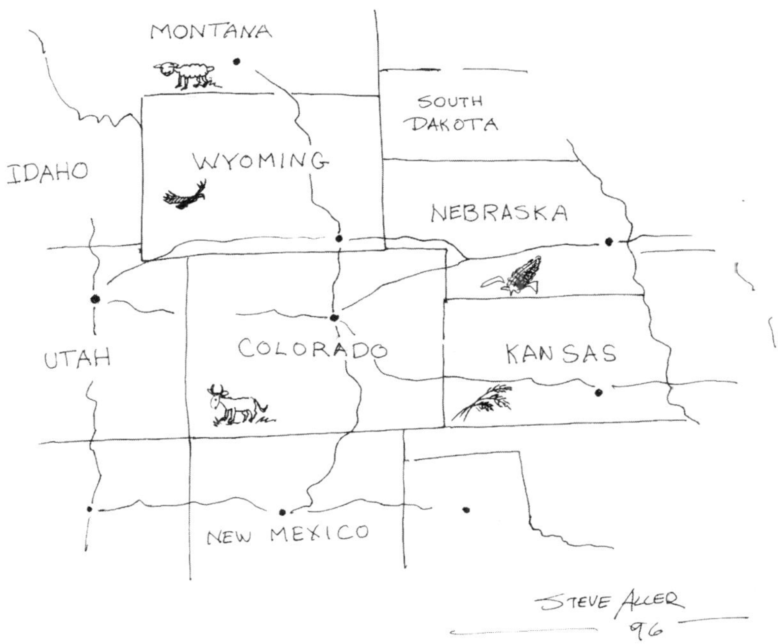

Gettin' Modern

Sam couldn't believe his eyes as his old friend and neighbor, Joe, drove in the gate to his ranch.

He'd called Joe yesterday and asked him to come over and help him gather his bulls in from the cows. Joe was good help and always showed up promptly to work. Oh, he was on time today, alright, but something was wrong. The old battered white stock trailer that always had a horse saddled and ready to go wasn't there. Why would Joe show up so unprepared? It just wasn't like him. As the pickup rolled to a halt Sam saw it. He saw it but couldn't believe what he was seeing. Setting there in the back of Joe's old pickup sat a brand new four wheel motor cycle thing.

"What in thunder is that and where's your horse?" Sam bellowed.

"Well, sir, you're a lookin' at the new way to

do things," Joe answered. "No hay to eat, manure to haul or fences to mend. Just put a little gas in it and it's good for hours. Then park it until you need it again. That's the modern way."

Sam shook his head as he walked away to get his horse and head out. When he returned with his horse from the barn Sam got his second shock of the day. There sat Joe on the "thing" looking like a little spaceman, decked out in helmet, gloves and even goggles.

"Safety equipment," Joe yelled back over his shoulder as he roared out of the yard in a cloud of dust.

"Well, it's sure faster," thought Sam as he loped his horse after the dust maker, by now far ahead. When he arrived at the starting spot at the top of the Big Gulch, Joe was already there laying in the shade.

"Ok, Joe, you know the routine," Sam instructed, "You go down the back side of the hill and I'll go around the front, we'll push the bulls ahead of us down to the meadow below and meet there."

After the usual eventful morning associated with gathering cranky bulls that really aren't looking forward to nine months of celibacy, Sam arrived at the meadow with his bulls. Joe was nowhere to be found. After waiting over an hour,

Sam started back up in the direction Joe should have come. Soon he came across a dusty, thoroughly disgusted, and embarrassed Joe walking the trail.

"I guess I found out modern ain't always best," Joe volunteered. "I needed the helmet because that "thing" was on top of me more than I was on it ! The gloves saved me from picking cactus out of my hands all the time after falling off. The only good thing was the goggles. Chewing tobacco at thirty miles an hour could get real messy without them."

"Where's it at ?" Sam asked between fits of laughter.

"Laying in a draw up there where the first bull decided he didn't like the noisy little thing. When he switched ends and looked at me face to face I realized I should have bought the model with a reverse. It didn't have one so I used my own. That thing was a hood ornament on a Charolais bull the last I saw of it!"

"If you don't mind, I'd like to go home and soak my body tonight. I'll be back tomorrow with the right equipment this time. I just hope my old brown horse will drag that thing back to the house so I can sell it. What do you suppose those things are worth with both handlebars on the same side?"

Free Enterprise

The cattle business has to be one of the last strongholds of totally free enterprise left in this country.

Even though we have tax laws, bankers, environmentalists and forest rangers to tell us what we can and cannot do, there still is a lot left up to our ingenuity. There must be as many different ways to make a living in the cattle business as there are people in the business. Everyone has his own twist to make a dollar off a cow. Some of these ideas border on genius in my book! A story related to me several years ago by a good friend was a classic example of one way to squeeze a little profit into our business.

The story centered around an old cowboy who lived almost a hermit's existence in an old cabin up a canyon. There were rumors he had once ridden with a band of enterprising young men who were into transfer of ownership of horses by night. Evidently age and brushes with the local law had driven him into the seclusion of his little shack in its remote location.

He bothered no one and appeared to talk to few. "Old Joe", as we'll call him, did seem to like my friend and my friend liked Old Joe. Since Joe knew every canyon, spring and rock in that part of the country, he was good help and often rode for my friend. In exchange, my friend ran Old Joe's few cows, tucking them away in some remote meadow each summer. The existence of the cows was to remain a secret at Joe's request. My friend helped brand the few calves each year. Out of consideration of Joe's shady past, he told no one about the little herd. Joe's little twenty acre spread couldn't support him otherwise, so my friend was happy to help the old man get by.

Eventually, Old Joe passed away, the secret of his colorful past locked away in his memory forever. While no one knew Old Joe real well, as is typical of a small ranching community, everyone came to the funeral to show their respects. Ranch communities feel it's their responsibility to sort of get the newly departed started off on the right foot for the next life.

There had been rumors that a daughter

existed in Old Joe's past, and sure enough, she surfaced at the funeral. After the services were over, the local ranchers gathered around to meet and visit with Old Joe's offspring.

As the group talked, my friend told the daughter about the small herd of cows he'd been keeping quiet about for Old Joe. Even though they only branded a small calf crop each year, he'd gather the little herd so she could sell them and get her meager inheritance.

Kind of shocked, a neighbor of my friend spoke up that he, too, had a few of Joe's cows he had been running on the sly to help the old man out! Another neighbor reported he also had a small herd carrying Joe's brand. Another and still another rancher added to the tally.

The final count showed Old Joe's holdings as well over one hundred cows! Run in small bunches, no one knew about the existence of the rest.

Old Joe had been producing over one hundred calves from his barren twenty acre spread! Now that's being resourceful and enterprising!

The Job

According to a study published in a book called "The Jobs Rated Almanac" we out here in rural America have some of the worst jobs in the country.

Our jobs as cowboys, farmers and ranchers are rated as the worst jobs in the land.

We always suspected that few people get rich doing what we do out here in these parts. Maybe it didn't pay too great but we felt the surroundings and the lifestyle made it all worthwhile. Imagine my disappointment to find out that we have the worst jobs in the entire country!

The ratings were based on salary (I'd have to agree on this one) stress, outlook, security and physical demands.

We'll pass on the salary question and look at the others. Stress. I suppose we have our fair share with weather, markets, loans and grasshoppers to worry about. Outlook and security may be a slight problem for us, but then today, who has any real security? At least if you've got some old cows out there to look after, you have a real steady job that will go on forever.

Physical demands may be a problem for us, however. A foot race of old cowboys over a hundred yards might have to be timed with a calendar instead of a stop watch. Horses on top of us, cows kicking our bodies and hours spent in all types of weather tend to take their toll.

Who has worse jobs than us, according to the list? Only seamen, fishermen, roofers, construction workers, and migrant laborers rate worse. We even rated poorer that NFL football players.

I worried what this bad publicity was going to do to the kids who want to grow up to be cowboys. I guess they will now have new heroes.

What is the best job to have today? Who will all the kids want to grow up to be? Are you ready for this? Number one was an actuary. That's right, actuary. I had to look that one up. An actuary is one who interprets statistics to determine personal losses due to sickness, disability or disasters. Honest, that really is a job and they claim it's a good one. Other "good" jobs are mathematicians, astrologers and computer system analysts.

I'll bet the kids of America have a ball playing actuary and Indians. I can hear them arguing, "You got to be the system analyst last time, you be the paralegal this time."

Here's some free financial advice. Sell your cattle and ranches. Use the money to invest in a pencil factory. These kids will need a lot of pencils to play with. And for Pete's sake, go get a good job. I think, though, I'll just keep on doing my poor old job. Darn it, I like it!!

A Real Cowboy

Greetings,

I need your help and assistance. In our 4th grade social studies class we are studying the Western and Plains states. We are reading and learning about the people who live there. The students want to know more about cowboys. Could you share with us what it is like being a cowboy today? Any help and information would be appreciated.

Thank you,
Ms. Pat Copley
8073 Park Avenue
Wayupthere, MN

Dear Ms,

First of all, I would like to remark on your first name. It is rather unusual, but very easy to spell. May I call you M for short?

Since I don't know if you are a teacher or a 4th grade student, I'll try to write very simply in case you are the teacher. Thanks for your letter asking about cowboys. You couldn't have written to a better person. I suppose I would be the model for the perfect cowboy. I'm over six feet four and weigh two hundred and twenty pounds with not an ounce of fat anywhere on me. (Notice only my head shows in this picture. What a shame!) Actually the picture doesn't do me justice since most people mistake me for John Wayne (even more so now that he's been dead awhile). I can ride anything (Ford, Chevy...you name it), shoot straight (heck, I got to the third level on Nintendo's Super Mario Brothers once) and dance til dawn (of course I do need a little nap between 9:30 in the evening until right before sunup). I drink the hard stuff (Pepsi with the sugar and caffeine).

Yes ma'am! I'm a genuine rootin' tootin' card carryin' cowboy. My nickname is even Tex. Actually I was raised in Louisiana, but I don't like people callin' me Louis!

Being a cowboy today isn't much different than back when Roy Rogers and his sidekick Tonto rode their white horses across the Ponderosa. My eyes are sharp and my mind is quick. This is necessary to avoid the dangers of trail life.

Us cowboys must constantly be on the look-out for hostiles (wives, bankers, and kids wanting lunch money). We have to keep our bodies in shape for the vigors of the trail. We have to endure long cold nights sleeping on the ground. (Actually it's not the ground, just the front seat of the pickup waiting for a rodeo to start.)

Well, M, I'd like to go on about myself, but I've got to go now.

Oh, by the way, did I mention that there's lots of horses I ain't been thrown from yet?

Another $uccessful Year

Well, Summer Rodeo Season is about over and I'm happy to report it has been another successful big dollar year.

Yep, that's right, a big dollar year for Texaco and Conoco, McDonalds, Firestone Tires, Ben Gay Deep Heating Rub and Pepsi Cola. These are all products I spent big dollars on this past summer.

It has been a profitable summer thanks to my personal efforts for Mountain Bell, Jiffy Lube and various shirt and jean manufacturers. I did my very best to support, in an extravagant manner, 7-11 (especially the people who make those petrified sandwiches), Taco Bell (for those times my wife absolutely refused to eat another Big Mac) and the Hershey candy bar people.

Included in my list of dependents for this year's income tax will be at least one rope manufacturer, a horse feed company and the

7 11
S. ALLER ©
96

neighbor kid who did my chores when I was off "going for the gold".

Thanks to my efforts there will be big Christmas's in the homes of people who manufacture Tide laundry detergent (thanks to a few muddy arenas), Band Aids, Tylenol and rain coats (I lost three).

I tried to see to it that there would be constant employment available for rodeo secretaries, hot dog vendors and people with badges telling me where I couldn't park.

I made rather substantial contributions to two different states for passing thru at a rate of travel considerably in excess of their recommended speed limits and one unnamed town received extra revenue due to a ticket for parking a pickup and trailer in an area not designed for that particular use.

All in all, it has been a successful summer for almost everyone I came into contact with. I haven't even gotten around to mentioning all the guys that won my entry fees or the gate admissions I had to pay for my kids so they could see Dad once in awhile.

In summary, it was a great summer that ended too soon. I hope all the above mentioned appreciate my efforts. I certainly appreciate them. Without these things, "going down the road" just wouldn't be as much fun!

If You Can't Say Something Nice...

"If you can't say something nice, don't say anything at all." That was advice my mother gave me years ago and I try to remember it!

Once in awhile, around my horse friends, it causes a few problems, however. If I followed her advice, while looking at some of their horses, there would be long embarrassing periods of silence.

You've all been there. Your friend just has to take you out to see his/her newest addition to the stable. On the way out to the barn he is running thru all the customary introductions,

"Yep, he's a son of the famous 'Old Boy', out of 'Oklahoma' by 'Truck'."

According to my friend, this horse just may be the greatest prospect since Secretariat, and probably will rewrite most record books. Still quoting pedigrees and dropping names, he disappears into the stall to retrieve this marvel of the horse world. In a few moments he emerges, lead rope in hand, ready for your confirmation that, whatever he spent to own this animal, was small price to pay.

As "wonder horse" reaches the daylight, you have to fight to maintain your composure. Many things cross your mind as your eyes gaze over the beast.

The door is too far way to make in one lunge, so flight is ruled out. As you go thru a checklist of responses, you consider, then discard the following ideas:

1. Faking a heart attack and hoping the ambulance and paramedics distract your friend.

2. Trying to imitate the sound of a pager so you can blurt out "Quick, it's the hospital calling, where's the nearest phone?"

Finally, you arrive at the conclusion that your friend is waiting for you to look over his steed and give an opinion...

Now, here's the dilemma. Whatever you say favorable, he will probably quote to others. If there are others present at the moment, whatever you say will reflect on your horsemanship.

As you allow your eyes to lovingly flow over his long weak back, down his small-boned crooked legs, to his totally useless feet, then up to a head that would look best displayed in a hunting lodge with moose horns attached, you search for an appropriate response that will take your friends feelings into consideration.

Finally, with the proper amount of awe in your voice you utter the perfect response, "Yes, sir, that is a horse!"

County Fair

No other single event out here in rural America gets everyone going like the county fair.

Mom packs up the quilt she has worked on nights after the kids went to bed. Depending on her self-admitted talents, she may also harvest the best from the garden and select the best jars of new canning to exhibit. Cookies get baked that you can't eat because they're going to the judge's stand.

The kids are the real center of the fair, though. This is the culmination of a year's preparation. (That part is theory only, however. Actually most of the preparation takes place about one week before.) Suddenly, record books come out to be done at 11:00 the night before the fair opens. Calves suddenly go into a crash program to get halter broke two weeks before show time. Lamb's diets get adjusted so they can gain or lose enough pounds to “make weight”. The neighbor’s ranch that has scales becomes the busiest place in the country as weights are checked on market steers, lambs and hogs.

There is a last minute flurry of activity as vet projects and electrical boards get finished. The local vet is swamped with calls to give the shots that were supposed to be given by now.

Right in the middle of it all stands old Dad — probably a frustrated, tired, somewhat confused Dad. He has irrigation water to set, hay to bale and cattle to check. That can all be done in between helping halter calves, build a new show box and run to town for more clipper blades. He may also be taking a crop sample in that he thinks just might be the best in the entire county, too.

Somehow, it all comes together and everyone and everything gets to town more or less on time. Then the fun starts.

I remember my days at the fair as some of the best of my life. After a summer of working at home and seeing few other kids, fair time was the social event of the year. I drank more pop in three days than I’d had all the rest of the year. Romances came and went several times a day during the fair. Everyone got thrown in the stock tank at least once during fair.

You got to stay up late and had to get up

early to get calves washed before showing. I loved it! I went through it as a participant, as a 4-H leader and FFA advisor, and as a parent. It's a wonderful time full of experience you will always remember. (Well, maybe a few you wouldn't mind forgetting!)

Watch for Dad standing around in the midst of it all, too. He's the one who's showing the most stuff at the fair. He's exhibiting his family, his livestock and probably his pickup and stock trailer as well.

Hang in there all you Dads. County Fair only happens once a year....Oh, of course, there's State Fair and Stock Show and ....

STEVE ALLER
96

I Can't Afford the Best

If you own a good horse, chances are you are on a first name basis with at least one good veterinarian. Inversely, if you have an inexpensive, kind-a-common, over-worked and under-pampered "stick" around, you may have the vets number written down somewhere, but you really can't remember his name.

The reason for this is simple. Nothing ever happens to a cheap horse, while everything happens to an expensive one.

I'll use myself as an example. Over the years I've owned lots of sorry horses. Oh, I got along with them OK, but I had to. No one would want them. They owed me a great debt because if anyone else had owned them, they'd be "ALPO" by now. But, however, they had the good fortune to be owned by me and thus assured of a long and easy life. The notable thing about all these “outcasts” were that they never got sick and they never came up lame. As a result, they never needed a vet. They also never needed special shoeing, special equipment or medication to keep them going. An example was a horse named Cotton. Cotton was a big, rangy horse with feet like dinner plates and a head that almost needed it’s own trailer. He was used hard and largely ignored. We vaccinated him when we remembered, shod him when we had time and fed him what we could afford. He had very few vet visits. All this neglect killed him. He was 28.

I should point out here, I had horses like Cotton because they were all I could afford. Finally I was able to buy the horse of my dreams. He cost more than most of the houses I’ve lived in.

Within a month of buying a “really good” horse, I entered the vet’s phone number in my telephone’s automatic dialer because I was calling him so much. The good doctor came for a runny nose. He came for a slight limp. He also came for a big limp. After a while, he just stopped by weekly because he knew something had to be wrong. He, of course, had to work in around visits from the special farrier we now needed and the chiropractor. I called him for every sneeze I heard. I guess I was paranoid but we were talking about “the horse”.

Good things did come from this relationship with Doc. For one, he got to buy a new vehicle with his newly found wealth. For another, I discovered his sense of humor. One day in a panic I called to describe my wonderful horse's latest ailment!

"Doc", I said, "his nose is swollen and so is his ankle. Do you think they're related?" thinking these must be the symptoms of some rare ailment.

After a pause on the telephone the Doc replied, "I suppose they could be if the dummy ran into something and then turned around and kicked it."

Finally the strain of owning the dream horse got to be too much for me. His special care was more than the other horses had cost. "Old Wonderful" went down the road. Now we are back to normal around here again. My other "common" horses just eat, perform and seem grateful to be here. They are on our "when we think of it schedule" and seem to be doing fine.

One sad note, however. I hear our vet had his new mobile vet clinic repossessed. I guess he got behind on his payments when his income dropped from not getting our calls.

A Real Shocker

Things get so boring around here at times that I find myself looking forward to just about any upcoming event. Going to the mailbox is one of those events that get to be important on slow days. This morning was one of those kind of days so you can imagine how happy I was to find two letters in the old road side can! My elation was short lived, however, when I saw they were both from the local utility company.

One, of course, was the usual first of the month bill. The other, however, I went ahead and opened. Inside I found this note.

Dear Customer,

Enclosed you will find a questionaire to be completed by someone in your household who knows the most about your electricity consumption. Please fill in all four pages of questions and return it to us so we can better serve your needs."

Attached was the questionaire, just as they'd promised alright.

Well, the one who seems to know the most about electricity consumption around our house would be our sixteen year old daughter. She doesn't seem to be able to exist without electricity. The minute her electric alarm clock wakes her up, her day is full of radios, T.V.s, blow dryers and curling irons. As she moves through the house, she has to turn on every light she passes. Yes, sir, she is the electricity expert in our household. But, she was gone to school. That left me to be the expert by default.

Before starting on the first question, however, I glanced at the second envelope, the bill. It was an electricity bill alright because it shocked the heck out of me! It also gave me an idea.

I sat down and composed this letter to the local power company....

Dear Sir or Madam,

I would be extremely happy to complete your questionaire. However, due to ever increasing costs of operating our household, I am passing these costs on to you. Please find enclosed a bill for answering your questionaire. You are being billed at the rate of two dollars per question plus a ten cent surcharge since the total time necessary for this project exceeds my usual attention span. Since my rates may change soon, an additional billing adjustment may be added to this amount at a later date.

One final thing. At the bottom of your questionaire is a space for suggestions. I would like to suggest you put any further questionaires in the same envelope with the bill. This would save you on materials, postage and labor costs. This would save you money, which of course would result in a lower utility bill for me.

Oh, by the way, I need to warn you. Next Saturday my daughter is having a slumber party here at the ranch. Is your electricity supply to our house sufficient to operate seven blow dryers, five curling irons and a boom box all at the same time? Please advise."

A (Short) Life of Crime

Rodeoing means long hours on the road and a very erratic meal schedule. Towns and meal time don't always match up. During one of these long "eating optional" trips I learned a valuable lesson — crime doesn't pay.

Leroy and I had been on the road for many hours. The absence of towns and needing to make an early morning pre rodeo slack had meant no stops for food. Leroy had been driving for several hours when we switched places and I took the wheel. No sooner had Leroy settled in the passenger side, he was fast asleep. Boredom and hunger soon were my biggest thoughts.

All day long there had been a paper bag on the seat between us. Since we were in Leroy's pickup and he hadn't mentioned the bag, I hadn't paid it much attention.

Now as I drove, it's presence began to work

on me. Leroy was asleep, anyway, so why not peek inside? Carefully I opened the brown bag and could not believe my eyes. There, like a gift from above was a large bag, opened, but almost clear full of lemon drops!

After pondering why Leroy hadn't mentioned them earlier, I decided he probably wouldn't care if I took some. At least if I was careful he wouldn't notice anyway.

At that moment I became a thief and it was wonderful! The lemon drops simply melted in my mouth. That pleasure far out-weighed the guilt at my newly found life of crime.

After I'd satisfied my hunger and gotten comfortable with my burglary skills, I decided to explore farther. Carefully, I opened the smaller brown bag I'd found next to the lemon drops. Maybe ole Leroy had candy bars in it. Instead, my heart skipped a beat as I saw, not candy bars BUT rat poison! My mind raced. Were the lemon drops contaminated? Were they poisoned bait? Did Leroy coat the drops with poison to attract the rats? I could be dying right now!

Even worse, I was going to have to wake Leroy up and admit my guilt! Maybe dying would be the best answer.

I woke him. Breathlessly I blurted out my confession.

“Am I going to die?” I asked.

Well, it’s a good thing I wasn’t dying because my funeral would have been over before my good (?) friend was done laughing. His concern was not exactly touching.

Obviously the drops were ok, but the rest of that trip had to be the longest I’d ever been on!

Should'a Noticed the Chickens!

I should have noticed the pen of chickens. They were a dead give-away, but I missed it. I thought I was so smart, but...

I suppose I really should start at the beginning.

For years I was a solicitor for a livestock auction. "Field Representative" was my official title, but door-to-door salesman was more like my job description. The way the job went was that on Monday you climbed in your car or pickup and took to the road going door to door across the dirt roads and winding paths that criss cross rural America.

"Hi, I'm Gary Hodgson. I work for the very best livestock auction in the state and to be real truthful, probably the best one in the whole world!"

I'd then try to convince these people that they should ship their livestock to our auction barn. I don't mind telling you I got pretty good at it. I learned the kid's names, their brand, where they ran their cattle summer and winter. In short, I learned everything that was important to them. I became their friend and people do business with a friend. Actually, I probably wasn't very good at soliciting because I did like these people and we truly did become friends in many cases. In fact, if they had a better idea for marketing their livestock than coming to my employer, I just drank the coffee, ate the cookies, gave 'em a free cap and told them I'd see them next year.

There was one step I haven't discussed yet. That was driving into a strange yard in a strange car and getting to the front door before encountering the ranch dog. It is hard to explain the stressful feeling of walking across a strange yard waiting for a growling fuzz ball to clamp onto your leg. Eventually, I got good at this, too. I learned to watch for signs of canine presence. There were obvious ones like a sign that said "Danger, Dog".

The not so obvious ones were the half eaten carcus of a very large animal laying somewhere in the yard or a six foot chain link fence surrounding a very well trampled yard. I watched for these signs and planned my approach carefully. I even carried candy in my pocket for a peace offering if

I was trapped away from my car. I figured, heck, if I gave him enough candy, his teeth will fall out someday and then he'll be harmless.

One day, however, after checking for all the signs of dog habitation, I saw none. The yard was quiet except for a pen of chickens near the back door. Odd location, I thought, but hey, if they had cattle to sell, who cares. I'd almost gotten to the door when out of nowhere came the biggest, baddest, bittin'est hound I'd ever seen. In an instant, he had my right leg on his dinner menu. Fortunately, before he could totally remove it from my body, a man appeared at the door and called him off. Since suing a person usually ends the chance of getting to sell his cattle, our conversation quickly moved to other things. He, of course, wanted to sooth my feelings too, so he promised me his cattle to sell that fall.

As he walked me back to my car, I remarked about the pen of chickens near the back door.

"Well, sir," he replied, "we keep 'em there for the dog. You see, he gets kinda bored way out here so on the days a salesman doesn't come to the door, we turn a chicken loose for him to kill. Just seems to keep him sharp."

Yep, I should have noticed the chickens.

Necessity Can Be a Mother

It has been said, "Necessity is the mother of invention." Sometimes, though, necessity causes us to invent things that would not make our mother very proud of us.

A few years back, my friend Charlie and I decided to run a few cows together. Our plan was to sit thru all the nearby auctions and buy the "bargain" bred cows. We'd then run them until they calved and sell them that fall, turning a nice profit. On paper the project looked "fool proof". In reality, it soon proved us to be fools.

By hanging around the area auctions and buying the "cheapies", we wound up owning the misfit, sorry, cull cows from every herd in five states. We did have some uniformity to our herd. We could sort out a load of cows with just the rear half or their udder spoiled, another of just the front half. I believe we could round up a load of cows who would not claim their newborn and a load who gave no milk at all. In fact, any malfunction of body or brain ever known in the cow world was represented in our herd.

Worst of the lot, however, was a big black cow we came to call Mable. Charlie came up with the name. I never asked him why he picked that name, but there must have been a Mable in his life he hated very much.

Mable was mean, wild and worst of all, a fence crawler. She would not stay any place we put her. It wouldn't have mattered if she'd been penned in an oasis, belly deep in grass, surrounded for miles by burning desert outside her pasture. Mable would have left tracks in the sand. Fences only seemed to present a challenge to Mable. She'd go under them, over them or thru them. We should have sold her, but we couldn't keep her anywhere long enough to load her, plus, she had a big bull calf. Having a good calf has saved many a sorry cow and Mable knew it. The calf was good, but unfortunately he had inherited his mother's disposition. Whereever Mable went, usually at a high lope, right behind her was the big black calf. When we saw him, all we saw were dollar signs. Greed was our downfall.

Following our fortieth time of gathering, Mable and her calf we had a strategy session. We decided to put a yoke on Mable. To the shop we went and soon we had constructed our "invention". Made of sturdy steel rod, the two pieces bolted together, well padded, around Mable's neck. Two arms extended about 18" above and below her neck. For extra effectiveness we bent the ends of the arms forward a bit and sharpened them slightly. This widened profile would make it impossible for Mable to pass over, under or thru fences.

We thought.

During installation, Mable had to be roped and tied down. This did nothing for Mable's already sour disposition. It wasn't until we released the ropes and let her up that we realized our miscalculation. Mable, now madder than a wet hen, was armed with a formidable weapon. She looked like some big black prehistoric, two horned rhinoceros. As she circled the corral, armed and dangerous, her calf followed trampling anything she missed along their path.

About the same time Charlie and I decided we might not have had such a good idea, Mable ran in under a rickety old shed in one corner of the big corral. I would estimate her speed at about forty miles an hour when the top arm of our invention hooked one of the rafters supporting the roof. It sounded like a tornado had hit the building and the effect was the same. The building immediately was transformed into firewood, the longest piece about two feet long. Out of the rubble plowed Mable, the well padded battering ram still in place. About a half a stride behind her was the big bull calf.

When she hit the wooden fence on the other side of the corral instead of breaking one or two planks, her widened profile got all five.

As Mable ran off over the horizon, we grabbed our horses and headed toward the hole in the fence. There, amid the rubble that once was a fence, laid our invention, bent and broken.

Mable traveled about eight miles and got into a neighbor's cows. We agreed to leave her until he gathered that fall. In August, the helpful neighbor called to say Mable got snake bit and died. Our big bull calf, which we had never been able to brand, was never seen again.

I've still got that bent and twisted invention hanging out in the barn. It serves as a reminder when I think about getting inventive. It also is a l we had to show for profit on our cow project.

As for Charlie, our wives got kind of cranky after that project and we just sort of quit seeing each other much.

Confession Time

This story contains a confession. Like most confessions, this one is not easy to make. Only when faced with the certainty of getting caught did I decide to make it. Sooner or later, you were going to discover my secret, anyway.

I'm getting older. This revelation sort of hit me the other day when I found myself looking for my glasses...so I could read the rodeo entry information in The WRANGLER. "Oh, great," I thought, "There I am wanting to enter a rodeo and I can't even see the entry phone number without my specs."

This got me to thinking of other signs of getting a little 'long-in-the-tooth'.

You know you're getting to be an "older" cowboy when:

1. It takes longer to unfold your legs after a long drive than it did to fold the road map.

STEVE ALLEN
96

2. You find yourself explaining "team tying" to a group of skeptical young dally ropers who've never heard of such a thing.

3. You arrive at a rodeo and hope the calves are small and the printing on the ear tag is big.

4. One of the most important factors when selecting a new horse is whether he's short enough for you to get on.

5. Your idea of driving most of the night is to pull over about 11:30

(or)

6. You select a traveling partner who is young enough to drive all night.

7. You rarely get a back number that is larger than your age.

8. The only time a "buckle bunny" approaches you is to ask you to tell your daughter hello from one of her college friends.

9. You start entering rodeos so you can go in the coolest part of the day instead of having the best run on the cattle.

And finally, you know you're getting to be an "older" cowboy when:

10. You realize how much fun you've gotten from the sport in the past and start to appreciate every year you get a chance to keep it up!

In fact, getting to be an older cowboy is a pretty good deal. It sure beats the alternative! See you at the next one!

Everybody's Got One

You can find one on just about any ranch, farm or horse place. They vary in color and age but otherwise there are striking similarities. Chances are, you've got one, too. I'm talking about the ranch pickup. The old knock-around, drive anywhere, do anything, all purpose vehicle.

This is not the shiny, occasionally washed version that even gets put in the garage or the machinery shed. I'm talking about the one that usually sets outside near the shed or beside the hay stack. Actually, it's probably setting wherever the last person who used it left it.

Years ago, it came to the place in a role of honor. It was a source of pride. It was washed often, pampered and maybe even went to a prom or a wedding. Over the years things just sort of fell off it (and on it!). "Old reliable" got where it wasn't much to look at, but it always started.

The last time you tried to trade it in, the car dealer said to bring it back in on Tuesday. That's when the city picked up the trash. At that point it got a permanent spot on the roster at home.

All these vehicles have several things in common. They all get their oil changed every 50,000 miles or when none appears on the dip stick. They come in two colors, fresh dirt and old dirt. They are probably missing part of the chrome trim, at least one license plate and one inside window crank.

All four tires will be different makes and probably different sizes, too. The only mud and snow tire will be on the left front. The dash will be piled high with syringes, old medicine bottles, ear tags, pliers and an old traffic ticket warning you to keep it off the highway.

This pickup will be worth $250 according to the car dealer in town. It will be listed with the bank as worth $9,000. If it is supplied to the hired man as part of his salary, the boss will claim it's worth about $200 a month and the hired man will say it's worth about two cents.

In spite of all it's short comings, it still commands a place of respect around the place. It's the one that always starts on a cold morning. And it may have towed the new pickup into town to get the "on board computer" fixed.

In this fast-paced, changing world, it is good to find something that is stable and reliable. I guess as I hit "middle age" I kind of identify with these pickups.

Old Sam

Old Sam had always fascinated me. He wasn't much to look at. Kind of skinny, he might have been over six feet tall, but with his legs bowed like they were and his back hunched over the top of his old black hat probably didn't reach much over five and a half feet. It wasn't his appearance that had impressed me since I was a pup, however. It wasn't even that in his younger days he had been amazing on a horse, able to ride the broncs and rope with the best.

Nope, none of that was what I found so amazing about old Sam.

Old Sam was a horse trader. He had been a horse trader for over fifty years. In a world full of traders who came and went (some left in the dark of night), Sam had always been there. Trading horses is a tough business. Being able to find horses, buyers and checks who are all good is a pursuit that drives most horse dealers into depression, bankruptcy or other lines of work. While others burst on the scene and meekly slunk away, Sam had persevered. Now, I'm not saying Sam had gotten rich trading steeds, but he always had a good pickup and trailer and had paid for a nice little ranch at the edge of town. His checks were accepted more places than American Express.

Having spent my life around the auction business I'd seen hundreds of traders come and go. I'd even tried a little swapping myself, but my heart was never in it. How could old Sam make it work?

I used to stop by his place from time to time to discuss weather, the markets and see his latest inventory. One day I finally just up and asked him how he did it.

"Sam," I asked, "how do you make it trading when no one else seems to be able to?"

I guess Sam had decided over the years I posed no threat to him so he took a dip of Copenhagen and explained.

"Son," Sam drawled, "it's hard to make it on the usual margin you can put on a horse. Most traders only make a few hundred dollars off a swap, if even that. Once in a while you get to make more, but that's rare. You just can't handle enough horses to make a living on a couple of hundred dollars now and then."

"My secret is that I always have two prices for every horse I own. I always quote the prices to a buyer before he sees the horses. Let's say a guy comes in here and wants to spend $2,500. I'll take him over and show him that sorrel. He's worth the money, the man will have spent what he wanted, and I'll have made my two hundred dollars profit."

"Now, let's say another guy stops in and wants to know what I have. I tell him I've got one horse for $2,500 and one for $7,500. Now this guy would never buy a measly $2,500 horse, but wants to see the $7,500 one. I take him over to see the same sorrel. If he buys him, he'll leave happy since he spent what he wanted to. I just made enough extra to keep me going for awhile longer."

"What if he asks about the $2,500 horse?" I asked.

"I just tell him someone is looking at him right now, and I'm not sure if he's going to take him or not." Sam smiled, "It's important never to lie when you trade horses."

You've Gotta Have Style

Whether your particular addiction is riding cutting horses, wrestling steers or climbing aboard bulls, we all have one thing in common. We are all in the relentless pursuit of a "style".

Once you have mastered the basic skills necessary to fork a bronc or heel a steer you begin the effort of refining these skills into a pattern or style. This usually takes most of the rest of your life. Besides horse and rodeo people, golfers also know what I'm talking about. So do baseball players, skiers and just about anyone performing a skilled maneuver.

When I was about fourteen years old a gentleman by the name of Shorty Creede introduced me to the sport of roping calves. I suppose he took the better part of an hour to show me the way to throw my rope properly, pull my slack, step off, flank and tie. At the end of that hour he said, “There, that’s all you’ll ever need to know about roping calves. Now go spend the rest of your life tryin’ to get it all right at the same time.” His statement stuck with me but I’ll admit at the age of fourteen the significance of his comment evaded me. At fourteen you’re pretty much invincible, invisible and think you can leap tall building in single bound. In later years several broken bones would point out I wasn’t invincible. I did enough stupid things for the whole world to see to prove I wasn’t invisible and the building just kept getting higher and higher. Slamming into the first story wall made me aware my jump wasn’t all I thought it would be.

Work on it we did, though, didn’t we? Many of you, too, have spent much of your life to date in pursuit of that refining style. We watch others whom we admire and try to copy their style. What aspiring bull rider doesn’t want to have Tuff Hedeman’s flair? Most heelers admire Allen Bach’s flash. We take bits from here, pieces from there and attempt to put them all together into one clump that will become us. Some things work out, others don’t. I’ll never be able to walk off holding my slack like Troy Pruitt, but I do rope a calf like Tuff Hedeman. (I’m assuming he doesn’t know how to rope one, either.) Actually, looking like someone else has started to become less important each year.

As I develop a few more gray hairs, I have started to realize something about my style. It seems the older I get the more I start to resemble myself.

Less is More

"You get what you pay for," used to be a statement of fact. The more something cost, the more you could expect for your money. Well, it ain't necessarily so any more.

It seems today, the more it costs, the less of it there is.

I went to the hardware store the other day to pick up a roll of wire. Usually, I would pick up a roll of old-fashioned barb wire and be on my way. Today, however, I needed barbless wire for a fence near my horses. Horses, as you know, can not just stand inside a fenced-in area. They must stand in the fence. I figured I'd save a vet bill and save money on plain old wire without any barbs. Right?

Wrong.

A roll of wire without barbs costs more than one with barbs. What's the deal? Does the wire factory have to pay some guy to take all the barbs off?

Have you ever noticed that when they took the lead out of gas, the price went up? I seem to remember years ago, when they started adding lead to gas that the price went up, also.

Decaffeinated coffee is another case where it costs more to buy something with parts removed.

When buying a good felt cowboy hat, notice if you will, the thinner and lighter the hat, the more it costs. My wife's clothing, about half the size of mine, always costs more. Pickups cost more today than ever, but I suppose the price of plastic has gone up.

If you are starting to get the idea here, you can add to the list. When you go to the vet's for a bottle of medicine for the cattle or horses, which costs more? Usually the stuff in the little bitty bottles, not the stuff they sell by the gallon.

Personally I'm still intrigued by the barbless barb wire. I want to know how that little guy gets those barbs off. Does he have to unravel the entire roll of wire and slide 'em off the end or does he use his pliers to take each one off without disturbing the wire. I wonder how he gets paid, by the hour, by the barb or by the mile?

The Trade

It is time once again for that most dreaded of spring time diseases to strike cowboys across the country. Not flu, not pneumonia, not even the common cold. This disease costs the American cowboy and cowgirl much more each year. The disease? Pickup trading fever!

That's right, the "Curse of the Cowboy", the "Cowgirl Crud", that most fatal of maladies, the "urge" to trade pickups.

Through the winter, the mud-splattered old pickup served just fine. It hauled hay, pulled tractors to start, and hauled kids to school. Suddenly spring appeared and low and behold, we start finding things wrong with "old faithful".

Maybe warm weather makes the transmission noisier and the doors rattle more. Maybe spring gives us the desire to wash paint that won't shine anymore. It may be the ads in the newspaper for all the latest models. For whatever reason, though, we suddenly find ourselves dissatisfied with the same old pickup that was just fine two months earlier.

The disease affects the mind mostly. It causes changes in that part of the brain that rationalizes things. You can easily detect the symptoms of infected people. They say things like: "We can pay the fourteen thousand difference with the two miles per gallon savings on gas," or "A crew cab would really be nice for when we take your mother out for dinner some Sunday."

One of the most often heard remarks is, "Shucks, we'll have all these extra bills paid off soon, so the payment should be easy to make." This statement generally is observed in the more advanced, critical stages of the disease.

When the disease hits, our whole sense of values change. In March the steering was "a little loose", in May, it's "just too darn dangerous for you to haul the kids to school with". A two hundred dollar repair bill in February becomes "nickel and diming us to death" in April.

We suddenly discover we cannot live without a crew cab dually even though we've hauled four kids and the dog around for years in the old one-seater. The kids are too old to go with us any more and the dog died, but don't let a few technicalities stop you.

Now for most of you, you could get by one more year with the old pickup. I, on the other hand, just have to trade. Why, just the other day I had to have a new headlight put in old brown. Once those expenses start, they'll just keep on. I don't have any choice but to trade!

STEVE ALLER
96